THE
WRONG WOMAN

CHARLES D. STEWART

1st WORLD
LIBRARY
Literary Society

The Wrong Woman

Charles D. Stewart

© 1st World Library, 2009
PO Box 2211
Fairfield, IA 52556
www.1stworldlibrary.com
First Edition

LCCN: 2009923379

Softcover ISBN: 978-1-4218-8817-0
Hardcover ISBN: 978-1-4218-8916-0
eBook ISBN: 978-1-4218-8718-0

Purchase *"The Wrong Woman"*
as a traditional bound book at:
www.1stWorldLibrary.com/purchase.asp?ISBN=978-1-4218-8817-0

1st World Library is a literary, educational organization
dedicated to:

- Creating a free internet library of downloadable ebooks

- Hosting writing competitions and offering book publishing
scholarships.

Interested in more 1st World Library books? contact:
literacy@1stworldlibrary.com
Check us out at: www.1stworldlibrary.com

1st World Library Literary Society

Giving Back to the World

"If you want to work on the core problem, it's early school literacy."

- James Barksdale, former CEO of Netscape

"No skill is more crucial to the future of a child, or to a democratic and prosperous society, than literacy."

- Los Angeles Times

"Literacy... means far more than learning how to read and write... The aim is to transmit... knowledge and promote social participation."

- UNESCO

"Literacy is not a luxury, it is a right and a responsibility. If our world is to meet the challenges of the twenty-first century we must harness the energy and creativity of all our citizens."

- President Bill Clinton

"Parents should be encouraged to read to their children, and teachers should be equipped with all available techniques for teaching literacy, so the varying needs and capacities of individual kids can be taken into account."

- Hugh Mackay

CHAPTER I

Having made final inspection of the knots of her shoe-laces and the fastenings of her skirt, Janet turned toward her "perfectly horrid" oilcoat, which, as usual, had spent the night on the floor. As it would never come off till she had tortured her fingers on the edges of its big rusty buttons, she always parted from it on unpleasant terms, casting it from her; whereupon this masculine garment fell into the most absurd postures, sprawling about on her bedroom floor, or even sitting up, drunkenly, in the corner,—which latter it could easily do, being as stiff as it was yellow. This time it had caught by one arm on the back of a chair, and it came so near standing alone that it seemed to be on the point of getting along without the chair's assistance. As Janet stood considering its case, she turned her eyes toward the window to see what the weather had decided, and now she saw the farmer leading forth her pony. She went to the window and opened it wider.

"Please, Mr. Wanger, make it tight. He always swells himself out when he sees he is going to be saddled. Then, when he has gone a little distance, he lets himself in, and both the girths are hanging loose. That's one of his tricks."

She leaned farther out and made further observation of the weather. As the air was mild and the sky serenely blue (though you can never tell about a Texas Norther), she took Sir Slicker by the nape of his collar-band and dropped him out of the window to be lashed to the saddle; then she turned to the mirror again, and, having done the best she could with the hat, she went to take leave of the farmer's family, who, as she judged by certain sounds, were assembled at the front of the house awaiting her departure. But scarcely had she stepped into the adjoining room and shut the door behind her, when the buxom, blue-eyed Lena, rushing in from the porch, met her with a hug that was more like a welcome than a leave-taking.

"Oh, goo-o-o-bye, Miss Janey. I am so-o-o sorry. I t'ink you are so-o-o sweet and nice."

And then Lena, whose open Swiss nature was either at the summit of happiness or down in the valley of despair, regarded her ruefully for a space, and after one more hug and the shedding of two large healthy tears, accompanied her out to the porch. There the Wangers were waiting and the children standing in line to be kissed—quite as if she were a dear relative, or at least an acquaintance of more than four days' standing. Janet kissed them all; and having done so she proceeded to the hitching-post, followed by the entire family, down to little Jacob, who stationed himself at the very heels of the broncho, and was so far forgotten by them all, in their concern with Janet's affairs, that they did not think to rescue him from his perilous situation till it was everlastingly too late, the horse having by that time moved away. And then Jacob, who had been studying his elders closely, after the manner of his tribe, guessed the meaning of those farewell words which he had not been able to understand; and as she drew away he opened his mouth and bawled.

Her route, which lay forty miles before her with but one stream to ford, might be described as simply a fenced road on each side of which was open prairie and the sky; for, though this land was all private property, the holdings were so vast that the rest of the fence could not be seen as far as the eye could reach. As this gave the roadside fence the appearance of not inclosing land at all, but rather of inclosing the traveler as he crossed over the vacant waste from town to town, the stretch of wire seemed to belong to the road itself as properly as a hand-rail belongs to a bridge; and this expansive scene, while it was somewhat rolling, was of so uniform and unaccentuated a character in the whole, and so lacking in features to arrest the eye, that the road might be said to pass nothing but its own fence-posts.

For a while Janet's thoughts dwelt upon her experience with the farmer's family, the final scene of which now impressed her more deeply as she realized how promptly these good folk had opened their hearts to receive her, and how genuine was their sorrow at seeing her go; and this reflection imparted so pleasant a flavor to the world that her mind kept reenacting that simple scene of leave-taking. But when she had got well out to sea,—for that is the effect of it except that the stretch of wire puts the mind in a sort of telegraphic touch with the world,—she drifted along contemplating the prairie at large, all putting forth in spring flowers, and for a time she seemed to have ridden quite out of the Past; but finally, recalling her affairs, her mind projected itself forward and she fell to wondering what the Future might have in store.

There was nothing to answer her, and little to interrupt her speculations. About the middle of the forenoon, or later, she encountered a fellow-traveler in the person of a cowboy on a bay pony. At first a mere speck in the distance, he grew steadily on her vision, and then went riding past, life-size and lifting his sombrero; which salute she acknowledged pleasantly, smiling and inclining her head. A very strong fellow, she thought, whoever he might be. A while later, as she was jogging along with her mind on the horse, whose need of a drink was now a matter of growing concern to her, she came to where a wooden gate opened upon the roadside, and here, after a moment of doubtful consideration, she entered; and having closed it and got into the saddle again by means of its bars, she struck out across the prairie with the intention of casting about until she should come upon one of those spring-fed water-holes which are always to be found, here and there, upon the cattle range. For a time it looked as if her horse would have to go thirsty; but just when she was beginning to feel that she must not venture farther, she found herself upon a slight rise or swell from which she made out a group of cattle in the distance, and with this promise of success before her she put her horse to a gallop and set out for it, slapping him with the reins. Presently, the ring of black muck becoming plainly visible, she knew her quest was at an end; and her thirsty animal quickened his pace as if he caught scent of the water.

There now ensued a course of conduct upon the part of the horse which was strange. There was a small mesquite bush near the water-hole which lay directly in the horse's course, and Janet, seeing he was almost upon it, and not wishing him to leap it, as a running cow-pony will often do, gave the reins a jerk to make him dodge it, the which he did, and that with a suddenness which only a cow-pony would be capable of. A cowboy's horse is so used to outdodging wild cattle that such a sudden turn is nothing to him. But now, instead of going to drink, he gave a leap and broke into a mad race, splashing right through one end of the water-hole and continuing onward. It was such a burst of speed as only the wildest rider could have roused him to; and he kept it up despite Janet's efforts to stop him. To her, it seemed as if no horse had ever gone at such a pace before. At every leap forward she felt as if he must shoot straight from under her. She supposed he

Charles D. Stewart

had taken fright at something; but instead of slackening his pace as he got farther away, he rather added to his speed like a horse in a race. Though there was nothing ahead which he seemed to be going to, and nothing behind which he could now be running from, he did not abate his efforts; he pushed forward—

> As one pursued with yell and blow
> Still treads the shadow of his foe
> And forward bends his head.

Poor Janet, utterly ignorant of the cause, and knowing not whither she was bound, rode a mad ride to nowhere-in-particular. At times she pulled hard on the bridle, but without effect; he kept right on with her. She clung desperately to her seat. There was nothing for her to do but ride; and so many strange things seemed to have happened at once that she was almost bewildered. Altogether he gave her a ride which, in her own opinion afterwards, threw into insignificance the adventures of Mazeppa or John Gilpin, or even the experiences of the Ancient Mariner "alone on a wide, wide sea."

The reason for the horse's hurry would appear to be a very good one when brought to light and explained; and this we shall probably be expected to do at this point, an historian having no choice but to tell what actually happened. There had been a mishap in the saddle-bow. The bow is that little arch in front which, when the saddle is in place, fits over the bony ridge above the horse's shoulders. This part of Janet's saddle, instead of being made in the good old-fashioned way,—which consists in selecting the fork of a tree and shaping it to the purpose,—had been more cheaply manufactured of cast iron; and that part of the bow which clasps the withers and sits on the shoulders spread out in the form of iron wings or plates. The saddle, at some time in its history, had received a strain which was too much for it, and one of the iron wings broke partly across; and this flaw, hidden by leather and padding, had been lurking in the dark and biding its time. When Janet braced her foot in the stirrup and made the horse dodge, it cracked the rest of the way, whereupon the jagged point of metal pressed into his shoulder with her weight upon it. It was nothing less than this that was spurring him on.

A saddle-bow, into which the horse's shoulders press like a wedge (for it must not rest its weight on top of the withers), needs to be strong, because it is the part which withstands whatever weight is thrown into the stirrups in mounting or making sudden evolutions, besides which it takes whatever strain is put on the horn; in short, it is what holds the saddle in place. With a broken bow and girths that are none too tight, a rider's seat is but temporary at the best; and it is safe to say that Janet's ride was not quite as long as it seemed. With a broken bow a saddle must, sooner or later, start to turn,—and it is a strange sensation to upset while you are sitting properly in the saddle with your feet in the stirrups; it is impossible seeming; and with a woman, who is fastened more tightly to the saddle itself, the sliding of the girth on the horse's barrel is as if she were soon going to be riding upside down.

Janet, sticking valiantly to her seat and riding like a trooper, felt suddenly that peculiar sensation and had a moment's horror of she knew not what. The next she was aware of she had struck ground in some confused and complicated way and quickly got herself right side up. And while she felt that she ought to be dead or at least badly injured, she had done nothing worse than to crush down a lot of spring flowers. And there sat Janet.

Her horse, relieved of the pressure on the sharp iron, and

Charles D. Stewart

brought to a halt by her final desperate pull on the reins, was standing stock-still, his saddle askew like a Scotchman's bonnet, and his ears laid back. But scarcely had she located him when he began to pitch and kick, and with the surprising result that the saddle slipped entirely round.

This turn of affairs was hardly calculated to please a Texas horse. What this one thought about it, Janet very soon discovered; for however meekly his stubborn spirit had given in to certain things, he had *not* consented to wear a saddle on his belly; and this time when he pitched he seldom used earth to stand on. He came down on this hateful globe of ours only to stamp on it and kick it away from beneath him. Up he went and hung in space a moment as if he were being hoisted by his middle and came down with a vengeance that jolted a snort out of him; and up he went again, turning end for end and kicking the atmosphere all the way round. He was no sooner down than he went up again,—and usually with a twist which threw him over to another hateful spot, from which he flung himself as if it were hot. And all the time the hooded stirrup flew about like a boot on a boneless leg and kicked him fore and aft.

Thoroughly insulted, he pitched by a mixture of methods which amazed Janet; she ran farther back. Now she beheld a fine vaulting movement, going up with the hoofs together, opening out in midair and coming down repeatedly in the same place; and here he worked away industriously, stretching his loins with the regularity of a machine and hitting away at the one spot in space with his fine punctuating heels; then he settled down to a short shuttle-like movement, his forelegs out stiff and his head down. It shook the saddle like a hopper; and the stirrup danced a jig. In this movement he fairly scribbled himself on the air, in red and white. Finding that this did not accomplish the purpose, he went back to mixed methods a while and threw a confusion of side jumps and twisting leaps; and then, after a particularly fine flight, he came down with a heavy lunge and paused. He was standing with one of his own feet in the stirrup.

Janet would now hardly have been surprised to see him throw a somersault, as, indeed, he seemed on the point of doing at times when he stood up so high that he almost went over backwards. This time, after a moment of inaction, he reared again, and as he stood up with his hind hoof in the stirrup the girth strap parted and the saddle dropped from him. He jumped suddenly aside as if he were startled at his success, and finding himself rid of it he gave a final flourish to his heels and galloped away. The last Janet saw of him, he was going over a knoll with a cow running on before. He seemed to be chasing it. We are not at liberty to doubt that this was the case, for many a cow-pony takes so much interest in his work that he will even crowd a cow as if to bite her tail, and outdodge her every move. And so it is possible that Billy, finding a cow running before him, took a little turn at his trade.

Janet, hatless, her hair half-down and her chatelaine bag yawning open, had thus far given little thought to her various belongings scattered about in the grass; but now that the accident was all done happening and she saw that she would have to continue her journey afoot, her first concern was to get herself together again. Luckily the comb and the hatpin had fallen in the same small territory with the hat and were easily found—though the hatpin, standing upright amid the flowers, was hard to distinguish for a while; and the contents of her bag, having spilled almost together, were soon accounted for except a small circular mirror. This was very difficult, but presently she caught the flash of it in the grass and gathered it up also. And now, ascertaining the condition of her hair, she went to the place that had been made by her tumble from the horse, and seating herself in it tailor-fashion,

Charles D. Stewart

she set to work pulling out hairpins and dropping them into her lap beside the rest of her property.

Having her hair in shape, she took up the hat. This part of her apparel, which had been stepped on without detriment but needed brushing, might be described as a man's hat in the sense that its maker had not intended it for a young lady. It was a black hat, of soft felt, with a wide flat rim which had been turned up in front and fastened with a breastpin, a measure which had obviously been taken because the rim caught the wind in such a way as to cause it to blow down over the eyes—a thing which a true sombrero would not do. When she had furbished it and put it on, she glanced at the image of herself in her lap, and then, having held the little mirror at a distance to better view the effect, she took it off and set to work with pins, making it three-cornered. This proved to be quite a change; for whatever it might be said to look like in her hands, it became a hat the moment she put it on; it had an appearance and an air; and now the dark surface lent itself all to contrast with her light, soft-hued hair and clear, delicate skin. It was still further improved, when, having removed it again, she set it on at a rakish artillery angle. Possibly, if hers had been the dark, nut-brown beauty, she would have seen that she looked best lurking beneath its sombre shade, and therefore have turned the rim down some way to even increase the shade; but Janet fitted that which was frank, open, and aboveboard. And so she used the black for contrast rather than obscurity—besides which there was another sort of contrast, for a soldier hat on Janet was a striking foil for her utter femininity. And its romantic pretense (so different from the dark gypsy-like romantic) was such an arrant little piece of make-believe that it had the effect of playful candor, acknowledging how impossible a man she would make; and while it was, strikingly, a pure case of art for art's sake, you could not but remark how much better *she* looked in it than any soldier could ever have done.

To tell the truth, we do not really pretend to know why Janet did this, or what taught her how to do it; anyway, she did it; and now, having so easily accomplished one of the most difficult parts of a self-made woman, she fixed it in position with the hatpin, snapped shut her chatelaine bag, and rose to go.

Looking forward in the direction she had turned to, her mind began to be crossed with doubts as to whether that was the right way. She looked in other directions. Then she turned slowly about. What she saw was simply prairie all the way round. Which part of that horizon had she come from—what point in space? There is nothing so answerless.

She was now in a world where there was no such thing as direction except that one side was opposite the other. There seemed to be nowhere that she could really consider as a Place! The spot where she had been sitting seemed to be a place; but now she realized that she could go far from it in any direction and still be resting in the middle of nature's lap.

How she strained her mind out to the very edge of things and tried to think! What endeavor she made to get out of her mind that which was not in it! She could not but feel that it was all because she was "such a fool"—for she could hardly believe that a whole country could be so lacking in information.

Poor Janet! She even looked up toward the high sun and wondered what kind of sailor science would compel him to divulge his relations with a certain wooden gate. But there was no recognition there, no acknowledgment. The four quarters of heaven were fitted together with a viewless joint. All was silent. Everything was a secret.

Of course she finally thought of the obvious thing to do; but

Charles D. Stewart

afterwards she was sorry that she did, for that was just how she lost a good part of the afternoon. She found traces of her horse's course—here some flower stems had been broken, and a little farther on, some more; and now that all was made plain she took her slicker, which was tied in a roll behind the saddle, and, putting her mind straight ahead on the course, she set out.

In his high gallop her horse had left no trail that she could follow as a path—nothing but slight records which might be discovered upon close and particular search. As his shoeless feet had made little or no impression on the sward, and there were wide spaces where flowers were sparse, she decided, in order to make progress, to go straight forward in the direction which had been determined, and then, if the fence did not put in an appearance, to refer to the trail again.

After a time, seeing nothing ahead, she began to look about, this side and that, in doubt; and now, being "all turned round" again, she looked for the trail. But she could not find it. Looking about everywhere, round and round and farther and wider, she at last found herself inspecting her own footsteps and following her own wandering path; and here she gave it up utterly. She knew she was lost.

Again she peered out at a point in space and wondered if *that* was the place she came from. How different the distance looked now from what it did when she saw it down that endless road. That, at least, gave some shape to the future; and though she had been in doubt as to what it might be like, she at least knew it was there. Now the future was all around her. A thousand futures now confronted her—all done up alike in blue and awaiting her chance move, this direction or that; whereby she may be said to have been confronted with the world as it is—a veritable old wheel of fortune. But she had to do something; and the only thing to do was to walk.

Making up her mind to the Somewhere in front of her, she simply went ahead; for the afternoon was going and the night was sure to come—a prospect that filled her with dread.

It is no wonder that Lot's wife looked back when she was well out on the plain. Probably she wanted to see where she was going—so Janet thought, as she trudged wearily along. Or possibly the poor woman wanted to make sure that she was going *at all*; for when you are walking always at the middle of things, and not coming to anything, there is no progress. Janet thought—for she had to think something—that she knew just how stationary Lot's wife felt when she was turned into a pillar of salt. Possibly, if the truth were known, Lot's wife desired to be turned into a pillar of salt— who can tell? Janet, walking along so unrelated and ineffectual, rather fancied that she herself might want to be turned into a salt-lick (she had passed one all worn hollow as the stone of Mecca by the tongues of many Pilgrims); because if she were such a thing she would not be so utterly useless and foolish under the eye of heaven. But still she kept trudging along, feeling the growing weight of the slicker in her arms, for Janet was not much of a hand to carry anything on her shoulder.

Janet walked and walked, but her walking did not seem to have any effect upon that endless land. The fence did not put in its appearance, neither did a house nor a path, nor anything else which would make it different from the sky-covered plain that it was. It persisted in being itself, world without end, amen. To make matters worse, her shoe began to hurt (she had suspected it would and taken the man's promise that it wouldn't), and the more she persevered the more it clamped her toe and wrung her heel and drew fire to her instep. But there was nothing to do but walk; and she kept on with her footsteps till the operation became monotonous. Still that roadless scene was unmoved. The

Charles D. Stewart

world was "round like an apple"; that she could plainly see. And as to her feelings, this globe was just a big treadmill under her aching feet.

The only escape from such tyranny is to rise superior to it, withdrawing the mind from its service; so she decided to think of something else. And now, as she went on with no company but her own thoughts, she had a growing realization, more and more vivid, of her fall from the horse and what the consequences might have been. It was a miraculous escape, due to no management of hers. Suppose she had been disabled!—and in such a place! What a thought! She became frightened at what was past. She had not really thought of it before; and now that she did, her imagination was thrown wide open to the future, and she looked into the possibilities ahead of her. A cow, she recalled, has been known to attack even a horse and rider. And these wild range cattle; how might they take the presence of a woman, never having seen one before? There were thousands of them wandering about this big place, with horns that spread like the reach of a man's arms. Her only recourse was to wish she were a man. This was a favorite wish of hers, indulged in upon those occasions when she discovered that she had been a "silly coward" or a "perfect fool." After all, she considered, a woman isn't much loss.

"And it came to pass, when they had brought them forth abroad, that he said. Escape for thy life; look not behind thee, neither stay thou in all the plain; escape to the mountain, lest thou be consumed.... But his wife looked back from behind him, and she became a pillar of salt." It was an old Sunday-school lesson. And Janet had to think something.

CHAPTER II

While Janet was determinedly putting her foot down on pain and keeping up the light of faith on the distant sky-line, another and quite separate horizon was witnessing a little incident of its own. On a spot on the prairie which was no more a particular place than any other part of it, a lamb was born. The two occupants of those parts, a man and a dog (not to mention a flock of sheep), were soon at the spot where it lay, its small body marking down in white the beginning of the Season. Nature had thus dropped her card announcing that lambing-time was now here; and so the little white form in the grass, meaning so much, claimed all the attention due to an important message—albeit the message was delivered with somewhat the carelessness of a handbill. The man stooped over and looked straight down with an expression at once pleased and perplexed. As coming troubles cast their shadows before, this little memento, coming on ahead of a gay and giddy throng, raised visions of troublous and erratic times. The dog, a genteel, white-ruffed collie, sat down and viewed the infant with a fine look of high-browed intelligence, as if he were the physician in the case. The lamb was an old friend of his—just back from nature's laundry. The newcomer, about a minute of age and not yet fully aware of itself, raised its round white poll and looked forthwith a fixed gaze as foolishly irresponsible as if it were a lamb that had just fallen off a Christmas tree.

Charles D. Stewart

The man turned and strode away, leaving the dog on watch to mark the place. Just below a water-hole near by was a place thickly covered with dry marsh grass, all combed over by the wind and matted down like a thatched roof, beneath which shelter opossums and rabbits ran about in tunnels of their own making. To this place he went, and having grabbed a handful of hay from the convenient mouth of a burrow, he returned to the lamb, and kneeling down beside it he rubbed it into a comfortable warmth and dryness. Not quite satisfied with the results (there was a touch of chill in the air), he produced a white pocket handkerchief which had not yet been unfolded, and he used this to perfect the work.

This latter touch was more than a Texas lamb can reasonably expect; but there were distant circumstances which prompted the act, and the sentimental effects of these were much augmented by the fact that the first and only lamb was disowned by its mother. She had given it a cold-eyed look and walked away without even the formality of taking its scent. As she was now back at her grazing again, it was plain to be seen that she was going to give herself no further concern in the matter; indeed, it was likely that when the lamb should come forward to make his claims upon her, she would resent and oppose such intimacy, sheep being different from other animals in this regard. The man felt, naturally enough, that the first-born of such a host, and the representative of so many idiots, mothered and motherless, who were soon to arrive, deserved a better reception. The lamb spelled Duty as plain as chalk; and so he rubbed away, with a look of weighty concern which almost obliterated the smile with which he began. When the fleece was perfectly dry and warm he stood up to await developments.

By this time the lamb, which had already tried to stand up, decided to do it. It got part-way up and fell. Again it came up on its stilts, wavered drunkenly and collapsed. It had made a mistake of some kind. But the only way to learn walking is to do it; and a lamb, being more ambitious than either a colt or a calf, rises at once and starts right in, regardless of the fact that it does not understand the machinery. This one was weak but game; and it went down only to rise again. It went in for a course of Experience; and finally, having got the hang of things, it was balancing on all fours with fair prospects of success. Its status was a little uncertain,—like a sailor just landed on a continent which seems to have been drinking,—but still it was up and ready to try a step or two if necessary. But now the dog, who had been keeping a sharp eye on every move, became so personally interested that he gave it a poke with his nose; and over it went. This must have been discouraging. The lamb, dazed for a moment, waited for the spirit to move it, and up it came again, a little groggy but still in the ring. It staggered, got its legs crossed and dug its nose in the dirt, but by using that for an extra support it got its bearings again and was not frustrated. This time it succeeded, its legs widely braced. With the general demeanor of a carpenter jack it continued to stand, for that way was solid and scientific; and now it looked straight ahead for the sheep that was not present. In her place was empty air—nothing. This not being according to the order of nature, the lamb was at its wits' end.

The man in the case, acting upon the philosophy of Mahomet, gathered up the lamb and went to the ewe—which would have been more easily done had the ewe been willing. Having caught her and made her fast by putting her head between his legs, which made very good stanchions, he hung the lamb across his palm and set it down carefully on the proper spot on the prairie; and now, everything being arranged as such things should be arranged, little Me went straightway to the point, his underpinning braced outward like the legs of a milking-stool.

Charles D. Stewart

With a well-filled stomach, the lamb stared out at the world in general, and seemed greatly edified. The man was about to let the ewe go, but hesitated, considering that after she got back among the multitude it might be quite a while before the lamb would have another chance. He had better keep her till he had made sure that the lamb could not hold any more. The lamb grew visibly in gumption; and finally, after another swig at the bar of life, he was a made lamb. He actually started to walk. His steps, to be sure, were rather theoretical and absent-minded, and as he had not yet discovered just where earth begins and air leaves off, he seemed to be putting his feet into places that were not there; but considering the dizzy height of his legs, and the unevenness of this wabbly world, he did as well as any lamb can do on one dose of milk. Once he seemed to be struck with the idea of having fun; he gave a frisky twitch to a leg and a sort of little jump-up in the rear. The man, satisfied with this evidence, let the ewe go, first taking the precaution to mark her by tying the handkerchief round her neck.

All of which took but a short while. A lamb, upon arriving, needs a few moments to take notice that this is the Earth; but he has not much more than come to a stop when he realizes that it is the place for refreshments. For this reason, the force of gravity cannot keep a good lamb down; and as nature has provided him with just enough strength to rise and partake, the sooner he is about it the better. After a few draughts from the fount of knowledge his education is complete; and it is not many days till sheep life is too dull for him and he must lead a livelier career. Mary's lamb "followed her to school one day," and the reason he followed her to school was (a fact never before published) that he thought Mary was his mother. It was a lamb whose mother had disowned him, leaving the responsibility to Mary. And if there were any tag-ends or trimmings on Mary's dress, it is safe to say that they bore evidence of having been in the lamb's mouth.

The present lamb, again deserted by its parent, was completely at sea; and not having anything to attach itself to, it simply kept on standing up, which was plenty of exercise for it just now. The man, having released the ewe, who went back to the flock with an inane *baa* which reminded a scattered score of other ewes to do the same, now turned his attention to the problem of carrying the little stranger. As this visitation was entirely unlooked-for, he had not brought the lamb-bag along, so he had to find some other way. His coat, unbuttoned at the top for the better insertion of his hand, he had been using as a sort of capacious breast-pocket in which he stowed his lunch and other incumbrances. One side of it now bulged out with the carcass of a cotton-tail which he had scared out of the marsh grass, together with various conveniences which he had brought along from the shack. These things out of the way there would be room for the lamb to ride; he therefore spilled everything on the ground and set to work to make an entirely new arrangement, pausing, however, when he had unbuttoned his coat (he had left his vest off) to observe the present state of his white shirt-front, one side of which, in addition to its generally soiled condition and the darker streak which marked the pathway of his hand, had now a crimson spot from the head of the cotton-tail. That side, in comparison with the spotless and polished condition of the other, presented a contrast as striking as did the new white lamb and the weather-stained flock. Having hung the rabbit to the canteen strap, he put the lamb in where it was warm; and now, as he resumed his ramble with the flock, the little grass orphan (or whatever we may call an orphan whose parents are both living) bobbed his head up and down at the powerful chest of his protector, and looked out upon the world with all the advantages, and none of the disadvantages, of having been born. This way with the young had previously been adopted by the aforesaid Mrs. O'Possum, who always carries the children in her pocket; and whom we may imagine noting the fact in terms of the very highest approval.

It had been his intention that morning to get back to the corral at an earlier hour than usual; and as the sun was well past meridian he ordered the dog out to turn the flock, the leaders of which were now about a quarter of a mile away. The collie, eager for work, skirted round and brought them all face-about suddenly, barking his threats along the van, and then closed in some stragglers, according to instructions received from the distance. The man stayed where he was till the flock had drifted past him; then he took his place at the rear again, the dog falling in close behind. He idled along after them, revolving in his mind his plans for the evening—some boards to be nailed tight on the storm-shed, and certain repairs on the south side of the pen.

Although the lamb had delayed him, the sun was still above the horizon as he drew near home—if a word which means so much may be applied to a herder's shack. A shack is a residence about like a farmer's smokehouse, being taller than it is wide or long; and as it is intended only for sleeping purposes there is just enough floor space to allow for a door, and room to turn yourself in as you shut the door. Its breadth is equal to the length of a Texan when he lies down in the bunk built into it, the headboard and footboard of which are the walls of the building itself. It might be called a bedroom on the inside, but as it is only a two-story bunk boarded in and roofed over, it is more properly a room-bed; or rather it is comparable to a passage at sea with its upper and lower bunk and the surrounding ocean of prairie—a sort of state-room in the flight of Time. The architect of this one had been short of lumber, or too economical, the result being that the present occupant was a trifle too long for it; and he had considered the advisability of cutting a little window in the side to let his feet out. Its inconveniences bothered him little, however, as he spent his evenings stretched out on the prairie by the fire. It was so far from being Home to him that he never felt so far from home as when he entered it; and as he seldom entered it except in the dark, it was hardly a familiar place to him. Outside it might be home all over; inside was a timber tomb and the far-away country of sleep. This edifice stood on a low knoll from the heart of which issued a small spring-fed stream which had cut itself a deep ditch or gully down to the general level; and on the slope opposite to where the stream went out was a narrow path where the sheep ran up. The little eminence, with its structures, was a shanty acropolis to a universe otherwise unimproved.

It was to this place he was at last coming, his blatant rabble moving gradually together as they neared their familiar destination. Now that he felt relieved of responsibility, his thoughts, which had hurried on before him, as it were, dwelt with much satisfaction upon a certain little prison-pen on the hill ahead. Once arrived here, the lamb, could get a meal from his unwilling mother, who would be confined in such straits in the narrow little pen that she could not move nor help herself. The advantages of this arrangement the lamb would make full use of; and thereafter he would get along very well, interrupting his slumbers at any time and supping to his full satisfaction. There was a row of the separate little stalls or sheep stocks along the outside of the corral, this department being the orphan asylum of the community; and hereabouts there galloped and capered, in springtime, lambs whose mothers had died in "havin'" them, lambs whose own mothers were too poor to support them, and most frequently the child of a ewe like this.

The sheep crowded still closer together as they reached the beginning of the sheep-path; and now the man's face may be said to have taken on two coats of expression—a stern judicial look with a smile underneath. The thought that he was about to execute Justice occupied his mind wholly as the

Charles D. Stewart

old wether led them into the strait and narrow way. With the object of catching the ewe, he ran on ahead toward the path, beside which he stationed himself, halfway up the hillock, just as the head of the column was coming; and when the misbehaved mother came trotting along he laid hands upon her and pulled her out of the procession. At this, the lamb, which had become a very warm spot on his breast, said something which sounded very much like *Ma-a-a*; whereupon he decided that it might as well have supper at once, after which it could follow afoot. The lamb, having been carried so far through life, came down rather carelessly on its newly unfolded legs and stumbled; but it soon picked up what it had learned of the laws of mechanics and fell to supper forthwith. The man held the ewe as before, and when he judged the lamb held a sufficiency, he hauled her away toward prison, pulling her unceremoniously out of the lamb's mouth. And then the lamb, instead of following, stood braced on the spot as if unable to comprehend that such a thing was possible. It let out a quavering complaint, a melting infant cry, at which the man stopped and turned his head, and, seeing it standing there and looking ahead in a wooden sort of way, he returned to get it, marching the ewe down the hill again.

"I hope I'll have five hundred like you," he said, scooping it up under his arm. "Yes, I do. You'll have me talking to myself yet. Yes, you will."

For a sheep-man to talk to himself is considered a bad sign; but the present hermit had no chance to go farther in this course. The dog, dashing suddenly ahead, stopped at the corner of the shack and growled. So occupied had the herder been with his distracting duties that he had not taken much notice of the shack as he drew nearer to it; but now that the dog raised the alarm he looked and saw a blue wraith of smoke hovering over the roof. His fire-hole, it seemed, was lit. This was not unwelcome news, as any one may imagine who has lived even a few days so utterly alone. But whether the visitor was a stranger or a friend was made a matter of doubt by the conduct of the dog, who was barking and growling and wagging his tail. And his only change in conduct towards his friend the enemy consisted in doing it all more industriously, making threats with one end of himself and waving a welcome with the other. But no sound came from the other side of the shack. The intruder did not stand forth and show himself. The herder wondered that his approach had not been discovered. In the meantime the ewe, which he had absent-mindedly let go of, had made her escape and was again mingling with the multitude which was now running pell-mell into the corral. It seemed strange that the person behind the shack did not step forth. Being now free of the ewe (who had in no wise thwarted Justice by her act), he proceeded to investigate his home. And when he reached the corner of the shack he saw—a Woman.

A Woman. At a sheep-shack. She had his tin stew-pan on the fire and was bending over it, sampling the contents. On the ground was a strange sight—two pieces of pie, two peaches, half a chicken, sandwiches,—some with ham and some with jam,—pickles and cheese. And the coffee-pot under full steam. The large-hearted and healthy Lena had put all this into the package rolled into the slicker. It was partly this that had made Janet's burden so heavy.

The man's jaw dropped, as almost did the lamb; but catching himself in time he hugged it closer with unconscious strength. The woman replaced the cover on the stew-pan, straightened up, and spoke.

"Good-evening," she said. This in a tone of positive welcome (possibly a little overdone).

Charles D. Stewart

"How do you do," he replied.

"I have just been making use of your fire-hole. And your coffee-pot. You see I was—I was—"

"Oh, that's all right. That's all right. Just make yourself right at home. Are the men folks gone somewhere?" He cast his eyes about.

"There are no—no men folks. You see I was just coming along by myself—alone—without anybody—any men folks." These words nearly choked her. But immediately she added, with the most brightening smile, "I was *so* frightened by your dog. He scared me so."

Having said this, she dropped her eyes to the stew-pan, the contents of which seemed to need attention just at that moment.

"Oh, he won't bite. Anyway, he won't bite you. He knows ladies."

"I am so afraid of them," she said, her eyes still occupied.

She needed a moment to recover her courage, thinking rapidly. And as for the man, he thought nothing whatever; he just looked. She was bright-eyed and fair and wholly perfect. She was dressed in plain black, with deep white cuffs which turned back upon the sleeves, and a white turnover collar, as neat as a nun. Offsetting, somehow, the severity of this, was the boyish side-sweep of her hair, and the watch-chain looped to a crocheted pocket on her breast. And on the ground lay the soldierly three-cornered hat.

To a man who had been expecting to come home to doughy hot bread and fried rabbit and solitude, this was a surprise. It was somewhat as if Providence had taken note of his case and sent out a Sister of Charity; and one who had the charming advantage of being also a dimpled Daughter of the Regiment. Once his eye had taken in the regular contour of her nose and rested on that dimple, his gaze did not wander. He did not even wink—it would have been a complete loss of looking. When she removed the lid from the saucepan a spicy aroma spread itself abroad. Dog and herder sniffed the evening air, sampling the new odor. It was a whiff of Araby the Blest.

"As I was just going to explain," she said, straightening up again, "I had an accident with my horse. I came in here to find a water-hole and he ran away and threw me off. Then I found I was lost"; and she went on to relate the details of her adventure up to the time of her arrival at the shack.

As she spoke, she felt as if she had been thrust out into the middle of a big empty stage to make a speech to that momentous audience of one man—a speech upon which everything depended. However panic-stricken she might be, she must not show it. For that would give him an opening for assurances, for allusions which would have to be recognized, for asseverations which would have to be formally confided in—intimacy. And that must not be. The least betrayal of fear by her would bring it about. There must not be even the suggestion of a situation. It had been a godsend that, upon the first failure of her courage, the dog had offered himself as a reason. The dog had made an excellent cover for her trepidation. And now it was a support to feel that the dog was walking about—an object upon which to saddle her nervous apprehension at any moment when she lost control.

She delivered her speech with a naturalness and ease which surprised her. She even added a little high-handed touch or two, referring to the aggravation of being thrown by one's

Charles D. Stewart

horse and thus delayed in one's business; not to speak of being made such an intruder.

The man stood and listened to the music of her voice. As she began to speak with so much ease, he was smitten with a consciousness of his personal appearance, with the four awkward legs dangling down in front of him. In hope of making a more manly figure before her, he set the lamb down, feasting his eyes meanwhile upon the dainty repast and the two white napkins spread upon the ground. And when he stood up again, no one knew less than he whether he had set the lamb on its legs or its back or stood it on its head. It now occurred to him that he had not removed his hat. He did so immediately.

"And as I was coming across the range," she continued, "I saw your place. I had been so tired and hungry that I had lost my appetite. A person does, you know. But I was just dying for a cup of hot coffee. So I decided to use your conveniences. And I intended to leave your fire-hole burning for you—"

"Oh, that's all right. I'm glad you did."

She gave a sudden little scream. This was so unexpected that the man, whose nerves were not easily touched, drew himself up straighter and stared at her in amazement.

"Oo-o-o-o-o!" she exclaimed, clasping her hands together and fixing her gaze upon the supper.

It was the lamb again. It was standing right in the middle of the feast, its legs spread as usual and one foot deep in the sugar-bowl. The lamb was waiting. It was waiting till the spirit should move it to the next idiotic thing to do; and it would no doubt have achieved it had not the man taken quick action. He seized upon the lamb precipitately and snatched it away; then he stood with one hand around its middle and its long legs hanging down, with the four hoofs together.

"Oh, isn't that a *sw-e-e-et* little lamb!" she exclaimed, delightedly. "Oh, *isn't* he a darling!"

"Well—yes," said the man, holding it out and regarding it critically. "It was certainly trying to be a sweet little lamb."

She blushed. She had not seen the lamb all by himself, before; and these were the first free and natural words she had spoken. After this spontaneous outburst she proceeded more guardedly.

"And after the coffee was on," she continued, "I thought it would be such a shame for a man to have to get his own supper after I had left, with so *much* to eat. So I intended to leave your supper for you. That is in case you didn't come along when I—I—You see I didn't expect you home so early." To which she quickly added, "You know, when I first came along, I thought the place might possibly be vacant. Of course, I had to go in and see; and then, as long as I had already made so free, I thought I might as well use your coffee-pot and things. And your coffee, too."

"Oh, that's all right—perfectly all right. This place doesn't all belong to me. There's plenty of room for everybody."

He delivered this with a sweep of his arm that seemed to give her everything inside the horizon, and possibly lap over the edges.

"So I did take your coffee—and sugar. And I hope you'll like what I have."

"Judging by the looks, it's mighty good. Perfectly grand. But I'll go now and put this lamb where he won't be scaring us again Miss—Excuse me, but I haven't asked your name."

"My name is Smith. Janet Smith."

"My name is Brown. Stephen Brown. Glad to meet you, Miss Smith."

He put his hat to his head in order to take it off. She acknowledged the formality with a slight bow.

"I'll go and fix this lamb," he resumed. "I intended to do some repairing before sundown; that's why I came home a little early. But it's rather late now to do much. There's other work I have to 'tend to, though. I hope it won't take very long."

So saying, he started away. When he had gone a little distance, and observed that the dog was remaining behind, an interested spectator, he called back: "Don't mind him if he watches you. His name is Shep. He likes ladies."

Janet finished setting Mr. Brown's table, which consisted of a place where the grass was worn short. When he was working among the sheep with his back turned, she patted the dog on the head with the greatest familiarity. Janet "loved" dogs. When next she looked up to see what had become of her guest, or host, he was disappearing in the deep little gully.

CHAPTER III

When the shack rose upon her vision, Janet's spirits gave a leap. A mere box it was, in the image of a house; but yet, from the moment its countenance appeared on the scene, that lost and lorn prairie seemed to have found a place for itself. The whole interminable region attached itself to the shack and became a front and backyard; the landscape was situated and set right, knowing its right hand from its left. Four walls, a roof, and a door—all the things necessary to make a threshold, that magic line across which woman faces the world with the courage of divine right. At the end of a lonesome, laborious day she saw it; and she hurried to it with a sort of homing instinct. Opening the door, she gave a start and stepped back. Another's "things" were in it. Now what should she do? It was a question with half a dozen answers; and they all said, Go.

Just outside the door was a box with a hinged lid. It contained kitchenware and supplies. There was the coffee-pot—and coffee. As there was no one in sight (rolling ground is very deceptive), she decided that, tired as she was and with the journey still before her, this opportunity of rest and a comfortable supper, with plenty of strong hot coffee, ought to be taken advantage of. Then, as soon as supper was over, she would retire from the scene and consider what was best to do. She would sit down and try her courage in the

Charles D. Stewart

dark. Possibly, under cover of night, she would come in closer to his camp-fire and sit there on her slicker. Or maybe there would be two men! But at present it was all undecidable, almost unthinkable; she must take this little respite from being lost and try to make the most of things.

The twigs of half-dried mesquite did not kindle readily. With fanning and blowing the fire consumed a great deal of time and matches; but at last it got itself into the spirit of burning. In the midst of these preparations she heard the bark of a dog and a medley of *baas*, and looking round the corner of the shack she saw that it was too late.

When Mr. Brown had recovered from his surprise and excused himself, she became very industrious indeed, flitting about on the little space of ground like a bird in a cage. Despite her confusion, her mother wit was still with her, prompting her to cover her agitation with the appearance of housewifely activity; so every time that she beat against the bars of her situation she carried a fork or a spoon or the lid of something. She set his place, fed the fire, put on more coffee. He continued to work about the corral. Though the sight of him was not quieting, she glanced up often enough to keep track of him. He seemed to take his time.

Janet, partially blinded by too much attention to the fire, looked up through the dusk as he went to the edge of the little gully and descended. He was a "full fathom of a man," and as he sank from sight his length seemed to go right down through the surface of things, like Hamlet's father retiring to the lower regions. When, finally, his head had disappeared, she dropped her pretense of being cheerfully occupied and turned her attention in another direction. She looked hard at the shack—its door half open and the two bunks showing. Her brows drew closer together, with the enigma between them. That little Home, to which she had hurried with such a feeling of relief, had taken on a different guise. It was now the place she must get away from. At the same time black night was coming on as if to drive her into it. The sun was sinking. In the east the vanguard of darkness was already advancing. She gripped her chin tensely and tried to think, her forefinger pressed deep into the dimple. On the upper bunk was a faded blue blanket; the lower one was red.

Which way should she turn, or how conduct herself? Dreading to go and afraid to stay, she was confronted with a problem the terms of which seemed only able to repeat themselves. With the terrors of the night before her, she dared not venture away from this man; her very nature courted his presence. His strength and fearlessness she found herself clinging to as if he belonged to her—and yet he was a menace! Of course there might be nothing to fear if—But If was the dove that found no rest for the sole of its foot.

The problem presented difficulty on every hand, as if things were on his side. The darkness and the shack worked together to prevent escape; they seemed to have her completely surrounded.

What sort of man was he?

Repeatedly she had taken note of his features, but only to feel more deeply how little can be told in that way. Her inability to decide what impression he *should* have made on her was tantalizing—the aching question still remained. The face is but a likeness; you should know the original. And yet his countenance, so strongly painted on her mind, seemed always on the point of answering her profoundest query. It was as if she knew him. She now contemplated her mental image more deeply, feeling that she could get behind that countenance and have absolute knowledge. But it was a delusion. The soul is invisible.

Charles D. Stewart

In utter homelessness she gazed down at that little space of ground allotted to him and her. And the supper which united them. In nature there seemed to be no barrier between man and woman; their paths led toward each other. The flat ground seemed paved with gradual ingratiating approach; and no defense but outcry—too terrible and too late. Surely too late, for he was in the position of her protector, and she would have to assume that he was a gentleman; and how is a girl by that prairie camp-fire going to say just how much room her person shall occupy? Then how shall she set safe bounds? With the darkness closing in around her she felt trapped.

Her wits hard-pressed by this paradoxical plight, she looked with new longing at the shack. She felt that if she were on the other side of that threshold, and it were hers by right, she could stand behind it with some assurance of power against him, some dependence in forces not her own. For a door-sill is definite, and on it rises a formal spectre; but the way to a woman's heart is not so. Out here there were no set bounds; nothing to give pause at a distance showing the first and fatal step: no line in nature which becomes evident before it has been passed. Without it the moral dead-line was too close. Oh! if that shack were only hers—the rights of its lockless door.

But it was not hers. Thus Janet's imagination battered at the doors of Home, scarcely knowing what she thought, but taking mental action, nevertheless, in the face of circumstance and the quick speech of things. It seemed to her— afterwards—that never till that moment had she seen the full nature of Home. That she could see any of its features, even for a moment, in a shack so frail that a boot could break it, did not seem reasonable, even to her; but the strength of a house is not all in locks and bars. She had caught the depth of the man's first charmed look at her. Even a shack can excuse one from the scene, extinguish the light of beauty, and then say with the voice of Society—keep out. Thus things do not so easily and gradually come to an issue. But before her was only the prospect of her open presence, without screen or barrier or warning sign. And she, on her part, had not failed to note that, besides his straightness and look of strength, there was something of virile charm. What a terrible thing to be a woman! So, having turned instinctively to the shack, and recoiled from it, and then, with nothing else in sight, returned to it with the imagination of despair, there was nothing left but to turn about and stand with equal bafflement before the closed secrets of his soul.

As if by a deeper instinct, rewarding her efforts, she saw in him certain abilities for evil—deep, deliberate, and daring. He had quite deliberately left her; then he had, as deliberately, and without saying a word, gone down into that place. The little gully was as steep, almost, as a grave, deep, long, and narrow. Her eyes turned toward its gloomy shape. What could he be doing down there? What thinking? She could hear her watch tick. A meaningless *baa* broke out in the corral and went round in changing tones among the sheep. While she is so standing, let us take a look at affairs in the gully.

Mr. Brown, upon arriving at the bottom, proceeded to cast a burden from his breast—first, a stone which he had been saving for an opossum, a rawhide thong, a newspaper which had done duty over and over, and which he kept in hope that it might yield up some further bit of news, and finally, the rabbit, all of which he dropped on the ground beside his hat; and then, getting down on his knees, he washed his face. Having spluttered vigorously into double-handfuls of water from the little stream and put the towel back on its bush, he turned his attention to his twelve-dollar boots—for in the country of boots and saddles the leatherwork is the soul of appearances. He removed the mud with his knife and brushed off the dust with the rabbit. Finding that this latter operation promised finer results, he damped the boots with the tips of his fingers, and taking hold of the long ears and hind legs he worked the rabbit back and forth so industriously that a fair polish came forth. With a careless twirl he threw the rabbit away. It was probably as well for Janet that she had no knowledge of what he was doing down there; she would have been terrified by these too evident indications of his intentions. Having combed his hair and brushed his clothes with the palms of his hands, he felt generally renovated and pulled together; he took his hat in hand and straightened up in readiness to make his appearance. Then he sat down.

Before him was the spring with night already in its depths. The little stream murmured of its flowing in the overhanging grass, and caught the color of the sunset as it ran out into the open. A little farther on it emptied its reflections into a pool of gold. Steve Brown, having in his mind's eye a vision lovelier than this, and much more interesting, rested his gaze on a dark spot which was the spring. At first, her presence at his firehole had seemed unreal; and yet perfectly natural. It was very much as if she had just stepped down out of the sky and said, "Your wish has come true." At least, he had been wishing that he had something fit to eat, having become dissatisfied with himself as a cook. His period of due consideration did not take long; he again picked up his hat, and after a momentary pause in this vestry or anteroom of the scene he made his entrance.

Janet, having done the last possible thing to the supper, stood her ground bravely as he issued from the trench and marched upon her camp; for so it seemed to her, so conscious she was of swinging thighs and formidable front as he advanced. He hung his sombrero on a nail at the corner of the shack, apologized for his delay, and stood with his arms folded, awaiting her orders.

"Sit right down, Mr. Brown," she said, indicating his place and smiling as best she could. She seated herself on the grass opposite.

"It is very fine weather we are having, Mr. Brown," she remarked.

"Yes; it was a fine day. Nice and bright; but a little chilly."

"It looks as if it might stay this way," she added.

"Yes—I think it will. Hope it will anyway. But you can't tell."

The last remark had the effect of bringing their beginning to an end—as if this pliable subject had broken off in too strong hands.

While she poured the coffee, he served the meat, which she had put at his place; and when he saw her take up his well-filled cup he lifted her plate at the same moment and passed it to her, giving and receiving together. In the midst of this exchange, Janet (probably owing to the ceremonious way in which he did it) suddenly saw into the little formality as if a strange new light had been shed upon it; and instantly she felt that if she had it to do again she would not set the table in this husband-and-wife way. She was smitten with self-consciousness; and thinking it over it seemed strange that she, who was so anxious to avoid all suggestion of intimacy, could have arranged such a token between them and not have been aware of it. In that all-silent place the act was like words—as if mere Things had spoken out loud.

Charles D. Stewart

"That is a pretty bouquet you have," he remarked.

The reference was to some spring flowers which she had plucked upon arriving and used to fill up her cup of joy, the said cup being one of Mr. Brown's.

"Yes; I thought they were very sweet. In looks, I mean. Especially that blue kind." Then suddenly, as the thought struck her, "But you see so *many* of them!"

For a moment he looked disconcerted, like a man accused of something. Inquiringly he looked at the flowers, first at the ones which belonged to her, then at the thousands just like them all around.

"But so did *you* see a great many of them." This was his defense.

"Oh, yes—Well—but what I meant"—the fact being that she did not know what she meant any more than he knew what he meant—"was—Of course *you* wouldn't pick them for a bouquet, though, would you?"

Instantly she felt that matters had been made worse. It was like offering final proof that he had not admired her flowers, really; and what was his defense?

"Oh, no—I suppose I wouldn't. That is, not for myself."

It was the first step of his approach!

"Some people do not care for flowers so much as others do," she answered hurriedly. "I have even heard of persons to whom the perfume was offensive; especially in damp, warm weather. Odors are always strongest in damp weather, you know."

It was a relief to feel that she had been able to lead away from it.

This put them on the weather again; then ensued a conversation perfectly inconsequential, and yet remarkable, to Janet at least, for the amount of guidance it needed. She felt, as if her fate depended on it, that there must be nothing of intimacy, not even suggestion. So much might come from the drift of the conversation. She kept it as inconsequential as she could—a sort of chat hardly worth setting down except great art had been shown in it. Had Janet been a more experienced woman, and one with the firm sure touch of the conversational pilot, there might be some interest in charting out her secret course, showing all the quick invisible moves that were made, and how she steered through swift hidden dangers and grazed imminent perils unscathed, chatting inconsequentially all the while. But Janet was not that. She was little more than a girl.

She did the best she could. Meanwhile the flowers flaunted their colors in the firelight, seeming now a danger signal to remind her of her bungling start. The flowers! She wished she had not plucked them or put them there. Those preferred posies, standing there apart from the crowd just like them, looked perfectly foolish. She did not understand what she had done it for. The moment she had made that remark she saw the only reason why he admired them: it was simply because they were *hers*. And she had almost pushed the matter to this admission, so thoughtless she was.

While they talked, she took fuller observation of him, hoping to find an answer to her great question. He wore a white shirt—this had flashed upon her first of all. Further scrutiny told her that he had better clothes than his calling would seem to allow, and in better condition. His suit was gray, and though somewhat worn and unfurbished, was evidently of

Charles D. Stewart

fine quality. There was little about his attire which would have attracted attention in a Northern city except, possibly, the wide-brimmed hat and the boots with high heels. He was about thirty years of age. In the shack shone a polished spur—there seemed to be nothing else of cowboy accouterment. She could not make him out. He seemed taciturn at times and eyed her strangely.

Conversation can take such quick turns. Words, even mere things, can pop up with such unlooked-for allusions. They had drifted into some remarks upon sheep-herding, a trying occupation. Mr. Brown attested its monotonous and wearing nature.

"Yes," she said, "it must be so. No doubt you are always glad enough, Mr. Brown, when the time comes to get back home again."

"Yes—I prefer town to this. But I can't exactly say that it is like going home nowadays. I have a house just outside of town on the county-seat road. But a house isn't home."

"Oh, no, indeed. But a house is a very good thing to have— even in this mild climate." She paused a moment. "But Texans," she added, "keep the windows open so much, night and day, that one might just as well sleep out of doors. There is no difference really."

Considered in all its bearings, this answer seemed an improvement; it encouraged her for the moment. But it seemed impossible for them to sit out there and talk in a man-to-man relation; they were Society. The very phrases of society,—even the flowers, the supper, the yawning shack,— everything, it seemed to her, was against it. It is in the nature of things; and the Devil is on the man's side. They were Man and Woman, sitting out there in that little circle of fire. It seemed to her at times as if some terrible light were being thrown upon them with a burning focus.

One precaution she tried to keep constantly before her. She must not tell him her affairs—nothing of her situation in the world. It did not seem advisable even to tell him the nature of her errand to the county-seat; too much might be reasoned from it, of her helplessness. Her great danger lay in being questioned: this must be avoided.

But strangely—and its strangeness grew upon her—he did not ask such questions. He did not seem to have the least interest in her family, her history, or the object of her journey. He asked where she was going, a conventional question, perfunctorily put. His remarks all seemed somewhat conventional. Even these she had sometimes to evade and direct into other channels; and naturally a conversation, conducted solely with the idea of concealing her affairs, did not prosper. He began to say less. Finally he did not talk at all. He simply listened. His quiet way of waiting for her to continue bore in upon her as if it were some new quality of silence.

To meet the situation she returned to the subject of her adventure; she recounted that day's travels with endless inconsequential comment and explanation. If she paused, he made some obvious observation and waited. Janet, rather than face awkward pauses, silences which she could hardly support, would take up her travels again. She talked on because there seemed no way to stop. His way of waiting for her to continue seemed quite in keeping with that deliberateness which she had already noted. What to make of it she did not know. It might be that he was simply satisfied with the sound of her voice. Or possibly he had not the least care as to her past or future. Simply disinterest! This latter feeling—despite the state of affairs was so desirable—

touched her in some deep part of her being.

She told herself he was full of studious design; but whenever he looked straight at her and repeated her words in his quiet, well-modulated tones, she found her better judgment softly set aside, and all put in obeyance [Transcriber's note: abeyance?]. At such times a pleasant feeling passed over her; all her speculations and apprehensions were sunk in the atmosphere of his presence. It was a soothing effect, a personal influence which extended about him and pervaded her part of the air. As she talked on and on, and he gave her attention, she felt it more and more, as if she were sitting, not merely in his presence but within the circle of his being. It was as if, with her eyes shut, she could have entered his company and felt its atmosphere like entering a room.

She had not been able to see any way of getting the immediate future into her own hands. Whenever she thought of bringing the story to an end, her mind confronted her with the question, What next? Something certainly would be next. With all her talking, she confined herself to the details of that one day's experience. It seemed capable of indefinite expansion; there would never be any end unless she made it. Having supported herself in conversational flight so long, she began to feel that anything was better than suspense. She must do something. With this in mind she ceased and looked out into the night. The stars, a vast audience, had all taken their places. She leaned forward and began removing the dishes from her napkins.

"It is time for me to be going," she said.

He sat up straight—as suddenly erect as if he had been caught sleeping in the saddle.

"Going! Going where?"

"I'm going—on my way."

"Why, town is seventeen miles from here!"

"Oh, I can walk if—if I only knew the way."

"And hear the coyotes? And no light!"

Getting his small heels directly under him, he rose to six feet and looked directly down on her. It was as if he had ascended to the top of his stature to get a full view of such a proposition. "Pshaw!" he said. "Stay right here. I'll fix you up all right."

Without pausing for further parley, or even looking to her for assent, he turned and went into the shack. From the inside of this sleeping-place there came sounds of energetic house-cleaning: pieces of property came tumbling out of the door—an old saddle-blanket, a yellow slicker, a pair of boots, a tin bucket. Finally a branding-iron bounded back from the heap and fell rattling on the door-sill; then there was a sound of wiping and dusting out. Janet sat silent, her hands in her lap. In a little while he came crawling backwards out of the door and brushed the accumulated dirt off the door-sill with a light blue shirt. He went in again, and after a moment appeared with the red blanket, which he shook so that it made loud reports on the air and then carried to the fire for inspection, and to find the long and short of it.

"I guess there isn't any head or foot to this, is there?" He smiled dryly as if this comment pleased him; and without expecting an answer he went into the shack with it and busied himself again.

"There, now!" he remarked as he came out. "You can fix up the little things to suit yourself. And if there's anything else, just let me know and I'll do it for you."

"I am very much obliged to you," she said, rising.

"Oh, that's all right—no trouble at all. And now, if you will just excuse me, I'll go and finish up around the place. If you want to go to bed before I get through, you will find a candle in the top bunk. I haven't got an extra lantern."

So saying he took his leave. He put three of the coyote lanterns on their poles at the corners of the pen, unwrapped the red cloth from the fourth and used it to light his way over to the shed. He came back, wrapped the red around it again, and hoisted it to its place at the top of the pole. A watchful ram *baaed* awesomely as it rose.

Janet's shoe had been hurting her unmercifully. She had not been able to compose herself in any way without in some degree sitting on her foot; and it had kept up a throbbing pain. As she stood up, it seemed to reach new heights of aching and burning. She decided that she had better take possession of the shack at once; so she got the candle and lit it at the fire. The first thing she did upon entering was to remove her shoes. The relief was a luxury. The door had no means of locking; the wooden latch lifted from the outside. Having latched it, she sat down on the edge of the bunk.

Her shack! But after a little this inward exclamation began to take the form of a question. Suddenly she rose and looked at the top bunk. The blue blanket was still there. She was very tired. After sitting a while in thought, she put the corner of the red blanket over her feet and lay down, letting the candle burn. She was sleepy as well as tired; but she kept her eyes upon the door. It was really his place, not hers. And that made it all so different—after all.

Of all our protectors, there is none whose rumorous presence is more potent than the Spirit of the Threshold. His speech is a whisper, and before his airy finger even the desperado quails. Thus doors are stronger than they seem, and a house, if there is no other need of it, is an excellent formality. The accusing Spirit stands aside only for the owner.

Janet kept her eyes half open, watching that ancient mark between Mine and Thine.

CHAPTER IV

Janet, opening her eyes upon daylight, sat up drowsily and looked about. How long she had been sleeping she had not the least idea. Her windowless chamber, all shot through with sunlight, presented a surprising array of cracks, and the slanting beams told her that the sun was well up. Her watch had stopped.

In the absence of toilet conveniences she arranged her hair as best she could; and having adjusted her skirt-band and smoothed out the wrinkles, she put her hand to the latch. Her attention was caught by certain sunlit inscriptions on the pine siding—verses signed by the pencil of Pete Harding, Paducah, Kentucky. Mr. Harding showed that he had a large repertoire of ribald rhyme. And he had chosen this bright spot whereon to immortalize his name. She opened the door and went out.

Mr. Brown was nowhere to be seen. The flock, all eyes, turned in a body and stared at her. Presently she went to look for him. He was not in the storm-shed, nor anywhere down the slope, nor in the gully. She walked slowly round the shack and scanned the prairie in all directions. The face of nature was quite innocent of his presence. The dog, too, was gone.

As she came back to her starting place, the sheep again regarded her in pale-eyed expectation. A ewe emitted her one doleful note; another gave hers, sadly. The fire had been burning quite a while; it had made a good bed of coals on which the kettle was steaming briskly. She put on the coffee and prepared breakfast; and as he still continued to be absent, she sat down and ate alone. Then she put up a lunch and stowed it in the pocket of her slicker. Its weight had diminished considerably from what it was the day before, and as it did not now have to be done up in the form of a bundle it could be carried in a more convenient way. She folded the slicker lengthwise and threw it across her shoulder.

He had pointed out to her the direction in which the road lay at its nearest point. She walked up and down restlessly. After much indecision and aimless casting about, she turned suddenly toward her own quarter of the horizon and set forth on her journey. But having proceeded a fair distance she slackened her pace and came to a stop; and again she strolled up and down, looking occasionally in the direction of the knoll. Finally, she returned to it and resumed her meditations, less impatient.

After a long time, or so it seemed to her, she looked up and saw him coming. He carried a rope, the long noose of which he was making smaller to fit the coil on his arm. As he reached the shack he threw down the coil and lifted his hat.

"Good-morning, Miss Janet"—he used the Southern form of address—"are you all ready to leave us?"

"Yes; I thought I ought to get as early a start as possible. I made the coffee right away. I did not know but you might be back in a little while."

"Oh, I had breakfast long ago. I went out to see if I could get your horse for you. But I didn't catch sight of him. I hunted for him longer than I realized. It is quite a distance for you to walk, and I thought we might fix up some way for you to ride."

"That was very kind of you, Mr. Brown. I shall be quite able to walk. It was only necessary for me to be shown the direction."

"The road is over that way," he said, indicating its position with his arm. "Keep in that direction a while and you will strike a wagon-trail. Then follow that and it will bring you right out on the road. After you get to the road, you will find a house about a mile to the right. That is, if you intend to go that way."

"I am from Merrill, Mr. Brown. I am on my way to the county-seat. For the past week I have been teaching school a few miles from Merrill. It is the little white schoolhouse near Crystal Spring."

"A teacher!" he exclaimed.

"I can hardly claim to be a teacher," she answered. "The girl who has that school was called home by the death of her brother. I have only been substituting. I am on my way to Belleview to take a teacher's examination."

As Janet offered this conscientious information, Steve Brown looked in vain for any allusion to her secretiveness of the night before. In her bearing there was not the least vestige of arts and airs, nor any little intimation of mutual understanding; she simply looked up with wide-open eyes and told it to him. This honesty, quite as if she owed it, gave Steve a new experience in life; and he gazed into eyes that charmed him by the clarity of their look.

"You are going to the court-house to get a certificate!" he remarked.

"I do not belong here in Texas," she said, continuing her story. "I am from Ohio. I am stopping with the Dwights, down at Merrill. But for the past week I have been stopping at a farmer's in order to be nearer the school."

"Will you be going back to Ohio, possibly?"

"It might be that I shall go back. But it all depends. I may get a school if I pass."

She stepped forward to take leave of him. But just at that moment he thrust both hands deep into his pockets and bent his gaze intently upon the ground, his brows knit together. She waited.

"Miss Janet," he said, looking up suddenly, "I would be interested in knowing whether you pass."

"Well," she said, "I suppose I might easily let you know."

"My address is Thornton, Box 20. I get my mail every day—excepting the last few days, of course;—but I will get it again promptly as soon as I am out of this fix I am in. I don't suppose—"

"Why, are you in some sort of trouble?" she asked, interrupting him.

"Not very serious. I need a herder. I really ought to have two or three for a while now. I don't suppose, Miss Janet, there is any *doubt* that you will pass?"

Charles D. Stewart

"I think," she said, a playful light now touching her features, "it is quite possible for me not to pass. I suppose I could have passed easily enough four years ago. But after I got out of the Academy, I went to live with my aunt; and women, you know, don't keep up their interest in algebra and things. This winter when Aunt Mary died, in Toledo, I came down here."

She stepped forward again and extended her hand.

He had been seeing more and more of beauty as he gazed into her eyes. The Truth was in them deeper than words. They were large gray eyes, gentle and quiet and soft as dawn; and they had that fulfilling influence which spread peace upon the waters of his soul.

"Good-bye, Mr. Brown. I am very much obliged to you."

"Well—good-bye, Miss Janet. Be sure and let me know."

She turned at once and proceeded on her way.

With her attention straight ahead, but without any landmark to go by, she went resolutely forward, and when finally she turned to look back she saw him standing just as she had left him. He did not seem to have moved. Again she put forward, widening the distance in imagination; and the next time she turned to view her work, the shack was sinking behind a billow of land. She stood now and gazed back at the flat, flowered expanse; then she turned her back upon it for the last time. One does not look long upon the gay curtain after it has closed upon the scene.

"I would be interested in knowing whether you pass." The morning had shed new light upon her situation; and this shed a light upon morning. And now that she could view her adventure in the light of its outcome, she went back to the moment of their meeting, and did so, recalling what next he said or did. She lived it all over again; this time more understandingly. Meantime the prairie accommodated her with its silence. It was the same sameness as on the day before; but not to her.

With her eyes fixed upon infinity she went buoyantly forward; for this time she was not lost. The sun, already high when she arose, was blazing somewhere in the regions above, and the strong light, flaring in her face and shining on the broad reaches ahead, was very trying to her eyes. After peering against it ineffectually for a while she took off the three-cornered hat and proceeded to undo her work of the day before, removing the pins and letting down the rim.

The wearing of a man's hat was one of those things which she herself would "never have thought of." But just at a time when she had been having experience with the tribulations of a big leghorn on horseback, she saw a woman with a man's hat turned up at the side; and the next day she had procured one like it, which she turned up in the same manner with a breastpin. And the leghorn, unsuited to trials of wind and weather, was left at home.

The woman—Raymond her name was—was passing the school on horseback, and she stopped in to get a drink. Janet noticed the hat more particularly because of its contrast with the woman's hair, which was light like her own; although, as she observed to herself, of quite a different shade. As it was almost noon she stopped for lunch, and Janet found her very good company if not quite to her fancy. She smelled horribly of perfume.

With the brim shading her eyes, Janet could now look forward with a degree of comfort. Presently she was brought to a stop by a small stream. It was a mere brook—probably the water from a single spring such as the one which issued from the knoll; but at this point it spread out and took the form of a wide patch of marsh grass. Farther down it gathered its laggard waters together and became a brook again. Janet, keeping clear of the bog, went down here intending to jump across. Finding it too wide for her, she followed it along, its varying width promising to let her pass. She skirted round other patches of marsh grass and black boggy places only to find it too wide again. At last she removed her shoes and stockings and waded it.

For some time she had been ignoring the troubles of her left foot, the instep of which felt as if some one had been heaping coals of fire on it. It was such a relief to step out of the hot grip of leather into the well-fitting water that she loitered a while in the current; then it occurred to her that here was the place to stop for dinner. With her slicker spread out on the bank she sat down and had lunch, holding her feet in the water while she ate. Being done she sat a while longer, and when the sun had dried her feet she put on the shoes again, lacing them carefully with particular regard to the ailing instep. Then she folded the slicker.

As she straightened up and turned to go, she beheld a Texas steer of the longhorn variety only a short distance away. He had been grazing toward her, and as she arose he threw up his head. At sight of him—he seemed to be all horns—she turned and made straightway for the other side of the stream. She splashed through it as fast as she could go; and being back where she came from, she turned upstream and ran. She kept on till she came to a particularly wide piece of marsh grass. Here, with a good bog between herself and the appalling pair of horns, she came to a stop. Her shoes were now heavy with mud and water.

Janet can hardly be called a coward for acting as she did. A

Texas longhorn of the old school was enough to move anybody,—better calculated to do so than either the elk or deer.

Consider the stag raising his antlers in the forest aisle. Held to the spot by this display of headgear you contemplate it in all its branches,—main-beam, brow-tine, bes-tine, royal and surroyal,—they are all beautifully named. To run is only second thought. No particular horn seems aimed at you. Between so many there may be room for escape.

But think of the Texas steer! To right and left of him is one long tapering tine. Each of them, naked as a tusk, has a peculiar twist which suggests that it is perfectly scientific. Immediately you are impressed with the idea of running.

He is a pitchfork on four legs. And so is his wife. With other beasts of horn and antler, it is only the male who is thus favored; he has them to fight out his differences over the ladies; and also, no doubt, to make a grand impression. But Mrs. Longhorn has them as well as he and is quite able to take care of herself. And so, meeting either of them in their native state, you are inclined to regard the horizon as one vast bull-ring. Janet was not at all cowardly when she arose and went.

Having reached a safer place, she turned her attention to the stream again; and as she was now confronted by the bog, she had to find a crossing somewhere else. Naturally she did not turn her steps downstream again.

The steer had grown small in the distance by the time she came to a place where the black bottom looked safe. She stepped in and got to the other side without difficulty.

For quite a while now, Janet's journey might best be

Charles D. Stewart

described by saying that she walked. The scenery was grass. Evidently she had missed the road. Still, though the fence was not yet in sight, she did not give up hope; a wire fence does not become visible at a very great distance. Her wet shoes were very annoying. The imprisoned water inwardly sucked and squirted at every step, and made queer sounds. Unable to endure it longer she sat down and took them off, and while they were draining, upside down, she removed the stockings and wrung them out. Although she did not get them thoroughly dry, the walking was somewhat natural again at least.

Her shadow became long and stretched out indefinitely beside her. The sun came down from above and appeared in its own form; then quickly it sank. She kept steadily on. She knew it could not be far now to the fence; and once she was on the road she would feel safer. But while she walked the gray of evening came on; then somewhere in the distance a coyote barked. Her courage began to depart, as the dusk deepened; it seemed to her as if all the loneliness in the world had come home to roost. It was no use to watch for the fence now; it would apprise her of its presence when she came to it. Regardless of the possibility of running into its iron barbs, she walked faster; at times she ran. A star came out faintly. It was night.

The swish-swish of her feet in the grass, the rustle of her skirts, became prominent sounds. She missed the company of her watch; she wound it up and got it to ticking; anything to ward off the solitude. The thought of camping out she did not like to entertain; but thoughts are unavoidable. Once she stood quite still to make a little trial of it, but her pause was not long; she soon got her feet to going again. She missed the sound of trees, the breezes playing upon them. If there had only been something,—she knew not what,—it would have seemed more world-like. There was an absence of everything familiar.

To stop and rest was now out of the question. It were better to walk and keep thinking of the road. That would be human ground. So she thought of the road and tried to keep her mind flowing in its channel. How far might it be now? How long?

In the midst of this suspense she sighted a light ahead—a camp-fire. It was somewhat to the left of her present course. Steadily it drew nearer, straight ahead—her footsteps had bent toward it. When she was beginning to distinguish the play of the flames, it sank from sight; but presently it appeared again, more plainly. Now a lantern was moving about behind a pair of legs. She could see just the legs, scissors-like, cutting off the light at each step. The lantern stopped and burned steadily; then another appeared. Then another.

The open side of a shed became visible, a block of deeper darkness which made the night seem lighter. Janet, scarce knowing her intentions, kept going towards it. The lantern which first stopped now turned red and began ascending. It was a coyote lantern. It was going up to the top of its pole. A sheep *baaed* with the suddenness of a bagpipe.

Janet halted. She had now gone dangerously near. The fire invited her to come; but many things warned her away. What to do she did not know.

To her dismay, the problem very quickly took itself out of her hands. The dog, alive to his duty, came out at her with alarming threats. A short distance from her he circled around her to make his attack from the rear, as Scotch dogs wisely do. Janet screamed and ran forward, though not so willingly as a sheep. As the dog desisted, in obedience to a sharp

Charles D. Stewart

command from his master, she halted again. One of the lanterns was suddenly lifted, and being held up to give a wider light it shone full on the face of the man. It was the countenance of Mr. Stephen Brown.

"Goodness gracious!" said Janet.

CHAPTER V

Rumor worketh in a thousand ways her wonders to perform.

On the day of Janet's runaway, Tuck Reedy, of Thornton, rode in at the southeast gate and struck out in the direction of certain water-holes, his mission being to look over some B.U.J. cattle which had recently been branded, and see whether their burns had "peeled" properly.

In a good many cases he found that the blow-flies had worked havoc, so that, working single-handed, he had a great deal to do; and by the time he had thrown a number of lusty calves and treated their sides with his bottle of maggot medicine, he had pretty well worn-out the day. Being done, he turned his attention to a cow which had become deeply involved in a boggy water-hole. He threw the rope over her horns and pulled with his pony this way and that, but without success. Finally, when the sun was going down on failure, he resolved to kill or cure. He gave the rope another turn round the horn of his saddle and started up at imminent risk to her neck. Her legs were rooted in the tough muck as if they were the fangs of a colossal tooth, but Tuck pulled it; and having now rounded out an honest day's work, his fancy turned toward the fire of the sheep-herding Pete Harding. Pete was a congenial spirit, even if he was not much of a horseman, and he had a pack of cards with which he passed much time,

Charles D. Stewart

trying to beat himself at solitaire.

Tuck did not know that Pete Harding was not at present in charge of the sheep. He eventually made the discovery by the light of Steve's fire; and he made it at remarkably long range. Like others whose vision has been trained on far-off cattle, he was very long-sighted; his eye could reach out and read the half-obliterated brand on a distant cow—a faculty which saves a horse many steps, especially on a ranch where the cattle do not all belong to one owner. Tuck, being one of this kind, was as yet afar off when he saw that there were two persons at the fire. Closer approach making the fact vividly plain, he pulled rein and came to a stop. Sure enough, it was a woman! She was sitting there eating supper!

The extraordinary spectacle quite balked his comprehension. Having taken in all visible details and circumstances, he very considerately turned his horse and made himself "scarce."

On the following day, while everybody was waiting for the mail to be distributed, Tuck was loitering up and down past the various groups on Thornton's principal thoroughfare. Coming finally to where the subject of horse was being discussed, he joined himself to this multitude of counselors; and finding Hank Bullen among those present, he related his experience of the night before. While the two speculated and conjectured, others became included in the conversation, a process which requires a story to be several times repeated.

"Did you say this was yesterday?" asked Ed Curtis, who had just caught the drift of it.

"Last night," said Tuck.

"You say she wore a white collar and cuffs and a black felt hat?"

"No; I didn't see what sort of a hat she had. She didn't have any hat on. I said she had on a dark dress with white around the wrists and a wide white collar turned down."

"I passed that girl on the road yesterday. She was going out that way. She rode a sorrel with one stocking behind and a star."

"Why!" exclaimed Reedy, "that must 'a' been the horse I seen out on the grass. He was a short-coupled sorrel with a stocking on his near hind leg, and he had a star. I thought to myself that he looked corn-fed."

"That's hers. She wore a man's hat. It was turned up on one side with a big breastpin. I noticed it wasn't any eight-dollar hat; she had to fix it that way to stiffen the brim in front. It was a black hat."

"She must be intending to make a stay to turn him loose like that," remarked Bill Whallen.

Further discussion yielding nothing but these same facts, the talk came round to horse-lore again.

A while later, Whallen, having called for his mail and received none, stepped out of the post-office and ran his eye along the row of horses at the hitching-rack. At the end of the row was an extremely starved-looking animal; and he was being stoutly defended by his owner, Al Todd, against the aspersions of the drug clerk.

"All that horse needs," said Al Todd, "is a little something to eat. What do you expect of a horse that is just out of the poor-house? There's a real horse. Look at his framework. Look at them legs. Look at how he's ribbed up."

Charles D. Stewart

Whallen examined the horse's bones and teeth; then he stepped back and took a general all-over view.

"What do you think of it?" asked the drug clerk.

"Is he for sale?" inquired Whallen, before answering.

"No, he ain't for sale," answered Todd. "This fellow thinks he ain't a nice horse."

"Well," said Whallen, "a man can easy enough put meat on a horse. But he can't put the bones in him."

"Nor the git-ap," added Todd.

"Does he know anything?" asked Whallen.

"That's just what he does," answered Todd. "I threw a steer with him yesterday and he held it while I made a tie. A steer can't get any slack rope on him. He surprised me."

"Who had him?" inquired Whallen.

"Don't know. I bought him up at the county-seat. He was one of them uncalled-for kind—like that suit of clothes they sold me up in Chicago. And Steve Brown says to me, 'I should say they were uncalled for, entirely uncalled for.' They can't fool me on horses, though."

"Say!" said Whallen; "Ed Curtis got in from Belleview yesterday. When he was coming along the road he met a girl on a sorrel. And last night Tuck Reedy—"

And Whallen went on to tell about the strange case of Steve Brown and the woman.

"Was he sure that was Steve Brown?" the drug clerk questioned.

"Reedy couldn't say it was Brown for certain; he didn't get a right good view of his face. He said it looked like him. But he could see the woman plain."

"Why, sure that was Brown," said the owner of the horse. "I saw Pete Harding when I was up at the county-seat; and he came along with me to see them auction off the bunch of strays. This horse was one of them; that's why he's so thin. I asked Harding who had his job now, and he told me nobody had it because Brown was running the sheep himself."

"How did the woman come to be out there?"

"There wasn't any woman out there when Pete left. I know Pete. Brown came out there to see how things were doing, and while he was there Pete remarked that sheep-life was getting pretty monotonous. So Brown told him to go away a while and give his mind a change. Pete didn't say anything about a woman."

"I guess Mr. Reedy didn't see very plain," remarked the drug clerk.

"See plain!" said Todd in disgust. "You don't listen plain."

"Then Harding didn't quit on his own hook?" queried Whallen.

"He didn't quit at all. He's going back in a few days if he gets through being drunk. He told me he had to get through before the lambs was born. He didn't know about any woman."

"Humph! Brown went off by himself and did herding like that before. He acts queer lately. He don't say much."

"That's what Pete said. Me and him trailed round Belleview all morning, and I got him to go along and bid in this horse for me. I saw he was a good horse, but I didn't know he was rope-wise. Look at his backbone. Look at how he's coupled up."

The drug clerk, having affected horse wisdom and miscarried, now stepped forward and began feeling the distance between the horse's rump and floating ribs, a move evidently intended to show his knowledge of this last technical term.

"What's all that for!" inquired Todd, with a touch of surprise. "Ain't them bones plain enough to see? I guess you think he is one of them nice fat horses that you have got to feel."

"That's right, Al," remarked Whallen. "Buy a horse like that and you see what you're getting. What's the use feeling when the package is open?"

The drug clerk, thus suddenly put out of countenance by the very bones he had been flouting, stepped back and held his peace; and presently, under cover of Whallen's going, he took his own departure.

Al, now that he had vanquished his opponent and made him seek the intrenchment of his counter, cast his eye about and searched the length of Main Street, one side and then the other. He expected to get sight of some one of the crew that had brought the cattle into the loading-pens; but they had totally disappeared. After looking into a few likely places, and finding that he had guessed wrong, he paused on a street corner to give the matter deeper thought.

"Come on, Al," said Toot Wilson, hastening past.

"Where at?"

"Up to the saddle-maker's. They're in there. He is making a fine one. Did you see it?"

"No."

"It's for young Chase. It's great work."

In John Diefenbach's workroom was a numerous company of saddle admirers, sitting and lounging about in the seductive odor of new-mown leather. The saddler, happily busied among his patterns and punches and embossing-tools, turned at times and peered over the rims of his spectacles in evident satisfaction. The heavy stock saddle, its quantities of leather all richly beflowered, was mounted on a trestle beside him. It was so near completion that the long saddle-strings now hung down in pairs all round, and these thongs, being of lighter-colored leather, and sprouting out of the hearts of embossed primroses, looked quite as if they were the natural new growth of that spring—in fact the whole flourishing affair might have been expected to put on a few more layers of leather out of its own powers of luxuriance. But there was nothing superfluous about it.

"What do you think of it, Al?" asked one of the company.

Todd looked it over, the broad hair girths fore and aft, the big cinch rings and strong stirrup straps. The stirrups were missing. His eye sought the hooks and pegs over the workbench.

"Do *them* things go on it?" he asked, pointing an accusing finger.

Hanging on the wall was a pair of Mexican *tapaderas*—deep hooded stirrups with a great superfluity of leather extending below as if they were wings for the feet.

"Oh! no, no, no," said the saddler, turning hastily and holding up his hand as if to quell this mental disturbance before it had gone too far. "These go on it—these." He held out a pair of plain wooden hoops.

Todd's countenance rearranged itself at once.

"She's a jim-dandy," said Todd.

With this verdict rendered, he seated himself on a chair which had a nail-keg for legs and gave his attention to the principal speaker as he resumed his account of a roping-match. The story was rather long, showing how it was that the best man didn't win.

In the ensuing silence Todd found his opportunity to speak.

"I just heard something," he said. "Steve Brown is herding sheep."

"That's nothing," said the story-teller. "He done that a couple of times before."

"And they say there is a woman out there with him," added Todd.

"A woman! What woman?"

"I don't know. Tuck Reedy rode past and saw them sitting by the fire. Ed Curtis saw her too."

"Whose sheep's he herdin'?" asked big Tom Brodie.

"I don't know anything about the sheep. He's out there tending them. And she's out there with him."

"I know what he's doing with them," said Harry Lee. "He's administrating them."

"What have they got?" inquired big Tom.

"Who's got what?"

"What is it that's ailin' them? I say, what have they *got*?" repeated Tom assertively, being a little in liquor.

"They haven't got anything. I said he is administrating them. When a man dies, the court chooses somebody that's reliable to settle up what he leaves. And this other fellow sees that everything is tended to and done on the square. They were John Clarkson's sheep, and they belong to his little boy. He is administrating them."

"Huh!" grunted Tom, whose untutored mind now needed a rest.

"But how about this woman?" asked Frank Sloan.

"She's turned her horse out to grass; and she's out there with him. Just him and her. All alone."

"Pshaw!" said Harry Lee. "They ain't alone. How could Tuck Reedy tell she was alone just by the light of the fire? There might have been somebody in the shack. Or behind it."

"And maybe the horse had just pulled up his stake-rope," said another.

"Or maybe the horse had hobbles on," added another.

"*Didn't I tell you Ed Curtis saw the same woman?*" said Todd, now growing assertive. "And she was going out there alone. And if there was anybody else around wouldn't they be eating supper with them? And if a horse was dragging a stake-rope wouldn't Tuck Reedy know it?"

To make the matter unquestionable he now started at the very beginning and told it all, going into details and pointing out how one witness corroborated another.

"You say she wore a felt hat? And was light-haired?"

"Yes. It was black. It was turned up at the side."

"Hell! I know who that is!" exclaimed Sloan.

"Why, that's a woman that was up here at Preston. Said she was an actress. She came along with a fellow and started a saloon over on the other side of the tracks near the loading-pen. After a while the women folks got to talking about the place and making objections; so then the rent was raised. I heard just the other day that she left town on a horse and was looking around the country. She fastened the side of it up with a big pin."

"A big breastpin," said Al Todd.

"That's her."

Here was a sufficient subject. Recollection failed to bring up a parallel. It was something new in sheep-herding.

"Well," said Sloan, finally, "a man's liable to end almost anywhere if he takes it into his head to herd sheep. They can raise all of them they want, but I'll stick to cattle; 'specially in spring. One thing about a cow or a mare is that you don't ever have to teach her the mamma business."

"Some sheep," remarked Todd, "ain't got natural human affections. When one of that kind has a lamb you've got to mix in and get her to adopt it. And half the time it's twins. And maybe she's willin' to take one and won't have the other. I wouldn't have the patience."

"Nor me, either," said Harry Lee. "I have a brother that tried it one time. And after he got through with that band of sheep, it would have taken Solomon to straighten out the family troubles. One thousand of them. Some had twins and some didn't have any, and the bunch was full of robber lambs."

"What's robber lambs?" asked Diefenbach, who had now turned his back on the workbench.

"That's a lamb that hasn't got any mother in particular. Maybe his own mother died or disowned him. And the other sheep all know their own lambs and won't have anything to do with him. You see, a sheep is mighty particular; no admittance unless he's the right one, according to smell. And maybe she won't take one anyway. Then the lamb is up against trouble; he keeps going round trying to get dinner everywhere. If he's a robber lamb, he finds out that if he comes up and takes his dinner from behind she can't smell him and don't know the difference. What a sheep don't know don't hurt her. That's where a lot of trouble comes in."

"What hurt does that do?" inquired the philosophic Diefenbach. "Hasn't a lamb got to have some milk?"

"Sure. But that sheep has got a lamb of her own; and pretty likely she has twins, and it's all she can do to keep them. So this lamb that's onto the game comes and robs them."

"You see, it's like this," put in Sloan. "Suppose you have a thousand sheep; and over here is a lot of lambs playing around. You see, a sheep and a lamb don't always go together like a cow and a calf. Sheep are awful monotonous, and I guess the lambs know it. So they go off in a bunch and have a good time. And when one of them gets hungry he lets a bleat out of him and starts for the bunch of sheep. They are all tuned up to a different sound; so are the sheep. And the lamb and the sheep know each other by sound. Well, the sheep will hear that and she'll let out her sound and get an answer back, and that way he'll find her in the bunch. Maybe they meet halfway; then she smells him and it is all right. Well, we have a thousand sheep all grazing together; and off here is a bunch of lambs with a lot of robbers among them, all playing and skipping around and having a hell of a time. Well, a robber lamb gets hungry all of a sudden, so he skips off and takes the first sheep that comes handy. He takes what ain't his. And maybe it's twins. After a while little Johnny and Mary come home and then *they're* up against it."

"And if you let things go like that," added Lee, "one sheep won't have any lamb or any milk and another will be feeding two twins and a robber. You can't raise sheep that way."

"But what is a man going to do about *that*? How can *he* help it?" pursued Diefenbach.

"Why," said Lee, "he's got to keep track of them when they're being born and see that every sheep takes her lamb and gets to liking it. Whenever there's one that don't want a lamb he's got to tend to her."

"*Donnerwetter!*" exclaimed Diefenbach, reverting momentarily to his native tongue. He picked up a beading-punch and turned to his own line of industry.

From sheep they got back to horses again,—conversation usually travels in a circle,—and being now in their native element they continued in one stay, discussing ways and means

"To wind and turn a fiery Pegasus,
And witch the world with noble horsemanship."

The story of the woman had reached this state, circumstantial and complete, when, by divers methods, it got out to the more aristocratic circles of Claxton Road.

CHAPTER VI

There was not a stone, it is safe to say, within half a day's walk of Claxton Road. Prairie country of the black-waxy variety is noticeably bereft of this usual feature of life, the lazy Southern ocean which formerly brooded over these parts having deposited black, rich muck till it covered everything post-hole deep. And so if a man had wanted a stone to throw he would have had to walk several miles to find one, by which time, of course, his anger would have cooled off. Originally there had been one here and there, but these solitary specimens, being such a novelty, and standing out so plainly on the flat scene, had been picked up by farmer or cowboy and taken home. Thus each of the several stones in those parts was engaged in holding open the barn door or the ranch gate, or was established in the back yard to crack pecan nuts on, much to the improvement of flatirons. If a man had stolen one and used it openly, he would sooner or later have been found out. But why do we speak of stones?

Shortly after supper, Mrs. Arthur Wright—Kitty they still called her—came out of the front gate whistling, and going to the middle of the road, there being no sidewalk that far out from town, she turned to the left and set out for the Chautauqua meeting at Captain Chase's. Claxton road, coming in from the county-seat, changed its name a mile or so out of Thornton and became Claxton Road. The Wright residence may be said to have been located just where the capital R began. At this point the barb wire of the prairie thoroughfare gave way, on the left-hand side, to the white fences of suburban estates with big front yards and windmills and stables; and on the right there came, at the same time, an unfenced vacancy, or "free grass," which, though it had a private owner somewhere, might be called a common. The estates along Claxton Road faced this big common, looking across it toward the cottages which marked the edge of town on the other side, and there was nothing to obstruct the view except a time-blackened frame house which, for some reason, had posted itself right in the middle of this spacious prospect. These places along Claxton Road were the homes of cattle and sheep-men who owned vast ranches in adjacent counties. They had thus herded themselves together, largely, if not entirely, on account of Woman and her institutions.

As the Wright place was the farthest out in this row of suburban estates, Mrs. Wright was frequently the first to start to a Chautauqua or other social affair; indeed, had it not been that she made a practice of hurrying up the others as she went along, she would usually have been the first to arrive. A short walk brought her to Harmon's, and here bringing to a hurried conclusion the Wedding March from "Lohengrin,"— an excellent tune to march by,—she changed her flutelike notes for a well-known piercing trill. At the second shrill summons Mrs. Harmon came to the door.

"Just a minute, Kitty—I'm coming."

"Don't forget your specimen," called Mrs. Wright.

Mrs. Harmon, after a somewhat protracted minute, came out with nothing on her arm but a book.

"I've just been too busy for anything," she explained. "You

know I had the dressmaker two days—I thought I'd take the opportunity while George was away at the ranch. And, besides," she added, after a short pause, "I didn't think of it."

"That's right, Statia. Always tell the truth, even as an after-thought."

"My! but you're coming out bright this evening," responded Mrs. Harmon.

"I hope we can depend upon the others," mused Kitty.

Mrs. Dix and Mrs. Norton came out of their respective homes empty-handed except for books. So also Mrs. Plympton and her mother.

"Well, I just don't care," said Mrs. Norton. "How in the world could I get a stone? I have been having the awfulest time with our windmill. The thingumajig that is supposed to turn it off has got broken or something and it keeps pumping water all over where I don't want it to. If I had an artificial pond like the Harmons I would know what to do with so much water. I wonder when Jonas Hicks will get back?"

"I wonder!" echoed Mrs. Dix. "I was depending upon him. Mr. Dix said he expected him back in a day or two. If it hadn't been for that he wouldn't have taken Fred along; for you know I can't put a saddle on Major myself. Jonas will probably be back to-day or to-morrow he said."

"I am su-u-u-ure," said little Grandma Plympton, in her sweet and feeble tremolo,—"I am su-u-u-ure that if we had all asked Mr. Hicks to get us a stone he would most willingly have done so. Mr. Hicks would do anything for a lady."

Grandma Plympton—what there was left of her after

seventy-four years of time's attrition—had a way of speaking which made it easy enough to believe that she had, in her day, been a beautiful singer. As her message to the world was usually one of promise and reassurance, she had the gift of dwelling with songlike sweetness on those words in which the music lay. She was altogether lovable and quaint. On fine days she would still go forth alone, bearing her mother-of-pearl card-case, and she would leave her card here or there as naturally as a flower drops a petal; for despite her years she had by no means turned traitor to Society. Nor had Society so much as thought of leaving her out. In her, indeed, the fine flower of aristocracy was still in bloom, and delicately fragrant.

The party, suiting their pace to hers, went more slowly after passing Plymptons', whereupon Grandma, finding herself thus accommodated, gave over what efforts she had been making and went more slowly still; and so, when they came to the Brown place, which faced the middle of the common, they were moving at a most deliberate rate. As they arrived opposite the small gate, they all, as if by simultaneous thought, stopped at once.

The object of their sudden interest was a rockery in the front yard. This work, a pile of smooth boulders about three feet in height, and as yet only partially covered with young vines, was the only scenic rival to the artificial pond in the Harmons' front yard. Steve Brown built it to please his mother, picking up a boulder here and there in the course of his travels and getting it home by balancing it on the horn of his saddle. During the last weeks of her illness, when her wandering mind went back to the hills of her girlhood, her imagination played continually around this mimic mountain of Steve's, and as it seemed to be the one joy of her prairie-spent life, he would carry her out on the porch in good weather and prop her up so that she could sit and look at it.

Jonas Hicks, becoming interested, took a hand in the work; he kept on making contributions as long as the resources of the country held out. Here was one reason that there was not a sole stone remaining to be discovered.

"If we only had a few of them!" suggested Mrs. Norton.

"Yes—but he might not like it," said the younger Mrs. Plympton.

"But we would just borrow them, you know," explained Mrs. Norton. "And anyway, how are we going to get along without them? Here we have arranged for the Professor to come and tell us about them; and we all promised to bring a specimen. It will seem strange for not one of us to have a rock."

"Oh, I don't think it would do any harm for us to borrow a few stones," said Kitty Wright. "I don't see anything so awful about it."

There came a pause of indecision. Mrs. Harmon—she was the dignified Daniel Webster of the circle, and just the opposite of the small and sprightly Mrs. Wright—was yet to be heard from.

"Really," she said, "we ought not to agree to do things and then not do them. We should have done it or else found somebody like Jonas Hicks to do it for us. What's everybody's business is nobody's business."

"And what's nobody's business is everybody's business," added Mrs. Wright.

"Good!" exclaimed Mrs. Norton. "Where did you hear that, Kitty?"

"I just heard myself say it. I did it with my little hatchet."

"Sort of a double-edged axiom," observed Mrs. Harmon.

"I am su-u-u-ure," chimed Grandma Plympton, "that if Mr. Brown were here, and knew the circumstances, he would most wi-i-i-llingly offer to assist us. Of course, we should never take—what does not belong to us, without the owner's permission, but I am qui-i-i-i-ite sure that if we were to take them and put them back just where we got them, Mr. Brown would quite approve of it."

"Mother has a very high opinion of Stephen Brown," said Mrs. Plympton.

"Mr. Brown is quite a gentleman, indeed," said Grandma.

This advice, coming from so white a priestess, and in words that lent so musical and sweet a sanction, removed the last mote of conjecture from the air. Mrs. Wright, as usual, was the first to take action. Every set of women, probably, has its recognized clown, she who is just too cute and killing. And those who do not like her say she is tiresome and "silly." Mrs. Wright, in keeping with the character, went through the gate with exaggerated show of dissolute abandon.

"Come on, girls," she said, breaking into the rockery. "I do hope I'll get one with feldspar in it, or something nice and interesting."

Mrs. Norton, having been the one to make the suggestion, now followed her own advice; Mrs. Dix, taking example from Mrs. Norton, came next; thus the motion was carried. And pretty soon the caravan moved forward, heavily laden with food for thought.

The next two houses in the line of march were those of Mrs. Jephson, and Mrs. Osgood and her sister Hannah—she was quite usually spoken of as Mrs. Osgood's sister; but the two latter had already gone.

"What do you think?" said Mrs. Jephson. "I just got word that Oliver wouldn't be home to-night, and he is probably gone for several days. And Captain Chase, too. The Captain had to go to San Antonio on business, and Oliver went along."

"The Captain, too! Not a man left in the neighborhood!" said Mrs. Harmon.

"Except Uncle Israel," added Mrs. Wright.

Uncle Israel was the Captain's aged darky.

A shortage of men was nothing new to the ladies of this community. Rather, being a cattle-raising country, it was a thing to be expected at any time in spring or fall; and when Claxton Road did enumerate its full quota of husbands, fathers, and brothers, many of them were liable to be absent from Chautauqua. Always with good excuse, however. One would be getting ready for a trip to the ranch; another would have to stay at home to instruct his foreman; another would have to sit up with a costly bull that was going through the rigors of acclimation; and on more than one occasion it was the very man who was being depended upon to tell them all about civil war or civil government who would have to be excused by his wife for some such reason, upon which there would be a chatter of regret and the meeting would fall into a conference upon matters in general. While the gentlemen would "expatiate and confer" with one another as to what breeding would produce the most wrinkles on a sheep's back (thus giving the greatest wool-bearing surface), the ladies would devise new wrinkles to make use of it. And usually the ones who produced the raw material would be entirely through with their plans while yet the consumers were settling fine points with regard to the finished product. In this matter of higher culture, the true bent of masculine nature was likely to betray itself in absence. But the present scarcity of man may be said to have been somewhat above the average.

For some distance the ladies went forward without saying a word. A spell of utter silence had fallen upon the party. Then Mrs. Wright spoke.

"Statia."

"Yes."

"Do you remember what we studied about gravity?"

"Why, certainly. Every certain number of feet a thing falls it goes twice as fast."

"Well, I have made a discovery just as good as Sir Isaac Newton's. Every foot you carry a rock it gets twice as heavy."

Some one among them dropped her burden; instantly they all let go. The boulders struck the road with almost as simultaneous a thump as when the drill-sergeant calls out "Ground arms."

"Oh! I'm nearly dead," said Mrs. Norton.

"So'm I," gasped Mrs. Dix, sinking down on the roadside grass.

"O-h-h-h!" gasped Mrs. Plympton.

The next minute or two was devoted to breathing.

"Why didn't you *say* you were nearly dead?" demanded Mrs. Harmon, when she had somewhat recovered.

"Why didn't *you* say something?" replied Mrs. Dix.

"Why didn't we all say something?" inquired Mrs. Norton. "I didn't know the rest of you were as tired as me."

Mrs. Wright, despite she was the smallest of the number, was evidently the hardiest; she had calmly turned her stone over and sat down upon it.

"It's a wonder you don't all blame it on me," she said philosophically.

"Well, whatever I learn about this stone I'll never forget," remarked Mrs. Dix. "Never as long as I live. Let's take them back."

"Yes; but it's farther to go back than it is to keep on," said Mrs. Harmon. "And we certainly can't leave them here. We are responsible for them."

A very evident state of affairs. Being begun it had to be done.

"Come on, stone, we're going," said Mrs. Wright, taking hers up again.

The others followed. Again the rock-laden ladies went manfully onward.

When next they reached the limit of endurance, Chase's big red gate was so near that they hung on with final determination, and when they were almost to it they rushed forward to get inside the goal before the rocks fell. They all succeeded except Mrs. Plympton, who lost hers in the middle of the road and then finished its journey by rolling it.

"I was never so glad in my life before that I am not a horse," she said.

Virginia Chase had come down the path to shut the gate, which some one among the earlier arrivals had not properly fastened, and she was the bearer of bad news. The Professor, after all, would not be able to be present. He had one of his sick headaches again.

"And who else do you think is sick?" added Virginia. "Aberdeen Boy. I wish Jonas Hicks was back, because Uncle Israel does not know very much, really, about stock. I am so worried. He held his head out so funny, I thought maybe it was something the matter with the ring in his nose. But it wasn't. He is just sick."

"I am su-u-u-ure," said Grandma Plympton, "that if Jonas Hicks were back he could give him something that would relieve him."

When the specimen-hunters had recovered from their labors they accompanied Virginia up the driveway, explaining, as they went, the whole case of the abducted rockery. In the Chase's big sitting-room the earlier contingent was drawn together in conversation as close as chairs would permit, and as the belated ones entered they were greeted with exclamations in which there was an extra touch of the joy of life, it being in the very nature of gossip to seek new openings and exploit itself in mystery and surprise.

Charles D. Stewart

"Hurry up, Statia; get your things off and come here—Wait, Mrs. Osgood; don't tell anymore till Kitty is here—Sh-h-h-h; be careful what you say before Grandma Plympton."

The newcomers, returning from the bedroom divested of their wraps, began at once to relate their own experiences in geology, but they had no more than stated the bare facts when they became aware that there was a more absorbing topic in the air. Somebody had told Mrs. Osgood's hired man, who had told his wife, who told Mrs. Osgood—but for that matter there was no great secret about it.

"Haven't you heard a thing about it, Mrs. Plympton—re-e-eally?"

This was asked by one who had herself heard of it only a few minutes before.

"Why, no; what is it?"

"You tell it, Mrs. Osgood. You can tell it best."

Then followed the story. In the course of its travels it had not suffered any loss of detail; it had rather prospered. Each person to whom it had been intrusted had sent it on its way richer and better; it became longer and truer. And so Mrs. Osgood told it, ably assisted by those who had just heard it and kept seeing new phases of it. Finally the case was rested.

"What do you think of it, Mrs. Plympton? You live nearest to him."

"I must say that I am surprised. But then, I don't know whether a person ought to be surprised at anything like that."

"And to think of it!" said Mrs. Dix. "Away out there where

nobody is likely to come along once in two weeks. What an idea!"

"Well," remarked Mrs. Harmon, who had been taking time, and might therefore be supposed to have given the matter her weightier consideration, "it is, in fact, just what one might expect. He has always been so steady and sober-minded. It isn't as if he had had a greater variety of interests and more social inclination and—wilder, you know. He was entirely devoted to his mother; and he hasn't the resources and flexibility to make so complete a change easily, and naturally."

"He has been acting quite strangely since his mother died," interpolated Mrs. Dix. "He cooks and eats and sleeps out on that kitchen porch, and doesn't seem to take any pleasure in being invited out, or spending an evening at other people's houses."

"That's it," said Mrs. Harmon. "In his position, and especially his *dis*position, a man is just ripe for the first adventuress that comes along. In considering such things we ought to make allowances."

"I suppose so," remarked Mrs. Norton. "But to think of it being *her*. The low calculating thing!"

Grandma Plympton was out in the dining-room with Virginia sipping a glass of wine, and having admired an embroidered sideboard scarf, a recent work of Virginia's, she was now engaged in examining other things as they came forth from a lower drawer, which creations interested her so much that Virginia went still deeper into the family treasury and finally brought forth a sampler and counterpane which her own grandmother had wrought. The examination of these things, together with reminiscence of her own early achievements, kept Grandma Plympton so long that by the time she reached the sitting-room the absorbing topic had subsided from its first exclamatory stage and was being treated in a more allusive and general way. Grandma soon gathered from the allusions that Stephen Brown had at last met the lady of his choice.

"Indeed!" she exclaimed. "Now I am sure he will settle down and make an excellent husband. Not that there was anything bad about him, not at all; but he was rather wild when he was a boy, and gave his mother a great deal of worriment—especially, I mean, when he took his cattle up into the Territory. And in those days she could hardly keep him from joining the Rangers. But now he is older and more sensible and has had responsibilities; and I am su-u-u-ure it will be a fine match for any young lady."

It is hardly in human nature to shatter such illusions. Thereafter, the subject of the evening was more guardedly treated, pending her departure. Grandma Plympton, valiant as she was in the social cause, could seldom stay up for more than the first few numbers of a dance, and she could never, of late, remain to the end of an evening party. Before a great while she signified her readiness to go, and after her usual courtly leave-taking she went away on the arm of her daughter-in-law.

"Do you know," said Mrs. Dix, "I hardly felt like saying anything before her. She is so old and innocent."

"Isn't she!" said Mrs. Osgood.

Virginia, much exercised over the health of Aberdeen Boy, had gone out to the barn to have a talk with Uncle Israel, who, with a peacock fly-fan moving majestically back and forth, was sitting up with eighteen hundred pounds of sick bull. Aberdeen Boy, a recent importation, and one of the noblest of those who were to refine the wild-eyed longhorns of Texas, was having no more trouble with acclimation than his predecessors; he manifested his illness simply by lying down and looking more innocent than usual, and heaving big sighs which wrung Virginia's heart.

In the sitting-room the study of Steve Brown went forward prosperously again, but especially now in regard to the woman in the case. If the one they named was anywhere within range of psychic influence, it is safe to say her left ear burned that evening. And when, finally, it was all over, the guests, departing, paused at the gate and turned their thoughts to the rocks there assembled.

"What will we do? I wouldn't carry mine for anything," said Mrs. Norton.

"Why, leave them here. We'll have Jonas Hicks come and get them," said Mrs. Harmon.

CHAPTER VII

Janet caught her breath and looked about her. It was the same shack on a hillock, the same gully and sheep-pen and dog, likewise the same Mr. Brown. Under the circumstances, it was natural for her to try to say something, and she did the best she could. When he had gathered, from her rather unexplanatory remarks, just what had happened, the first thought that crossed his mind was that he had eaten the last piece of fruit-cake which she left behind. If there is anything embarrassing to a man, it is to have company come unexpectedly when there is not a thing fit to eat in the house. He had finished up the cake a short while before, together with the remainder of crackers and a dill pickle.

"I have eaten up all the good stuff," he explained. "Do you like beans?"

"Yes, indeed," answered Janet, who was truly hungry.

He lifted the lid of the box and produced a small iron pot of boiled beans. They were beans of the Mexican variety, a kind which look nice and brown because they are that color before you cook them. When he had put some bacon into the frying-pan and given it time to heat, he scraped the beans in and stirred them up. He had made bread for supper by the usual method of baking soft dough in a skillet with the lid on; there was left of this a wedge big enough to split the stoutest appetite; and when he had placed this where it would warm up, he turned his attention to the coffee-pot.

"Oh, you do not need to do that. I can make my own coffee," offered Janet.

"You had better let me get supper," he answered. "You're tired."

Several times during the day she had pondered upon his high-handed way of taking charge of her affairs. Submitting to this further dictation, she spread her slicker before her place at table, as indicated by the bare spot of ground, and sat down. Mr. Brown took a bucket and disappeared in the gully. Evidently he had gone to get fresh water. Janet now put her feet out farther toward the fire.

When he returned, he made some remarks upon the weather and put on the coffee; then he turned about and went into the shack. As on the previous evening, everything came tumbling pell-mell out of the door. Janet, having nothing else to do, looked up and gave her attention to a big sixteen-carat star.

Shep, the dog, came and planted himself at the very edge of the bare spot. Without giving her so much as a glance, he sat there primly and looked straight off the end of his nose at the sugar bowl in the middle. Not till this moment had Janet realized what a beautiful, intelligent-looking collie dog Mr. Brown had. His brown-buff coat, of just the right shade, seemed slightly veiled with black; his full out-arching front was pure white.

"Shep," said Janet.

Charles D. Stewart

His fine eyebrow rose as he gave her a look—a very short one, however. When she addressed him again she could see his interest rising a degree; finally he came and sat down beside her. Encouraged by this show of friendship, Janet put her hand on him.

When her host had got through with the more violent exercises of practical courtesy,—which sounded somewhat like trouble in a barroom,—he came out bearing a jug marked MOLASSES; this he set down before her, and then, finding the coffee done, he proceeded to serve up the viands.

"That isn't much of a supper," he remarked, sitting down opposite.

"It tastes very good," said Janet.

It hardly did seem the right thing to set before such a guest. But Janet, as good as her word, steadily made way with the *frijole* beans and did full justice to the hot bread; and soon, inspirited by his powerful coffee, she continued the story of how she was frightened by the steer and baffled by the brook, and how she was foolish enough to think she was going straight forward all the time.

He had a way, whenever she came to a pause, of enticing her to go on. Sometimes he primed the conversation by repeating the last thing she had said; again, an apt word or two summed up the whole spirit of the matter encouragingly; or there would be just a composed waiting for her to resume.

Not that he had any difficulty in finding something to say. He evidently liked to hear her talk, and so he rather deferred to her. Whether it was that she now had a feeling of this, or that there was something in the influence of his presence, his voice and manner, which removed all constraint, Janet had not the least difficulty in talking. She told him how the teacher at the school "boarded round," what an unnecessary number of classes Miss Porter had for so small a number of pupils,—although it was difficult to remedy the matter by "setting back" certain children, because their proud mothers would object to such a leveling,—and how the Blodgett children, four of them, all came to school on the back of one buckskin pony, the youngest having to hold on tight to keep from slipping off at the tail. "Buckskin,"; it seemed, had won quite a place in Janet's affections, although he was the worst behaved horse that came to school. He used to graze in the yard till school was out,—the other horses being staked out on the prairie,—and he had become so familiar that he would sometimes go so far as to put his head in at the window in hope of being fed. And Janet could not see, considering that Texas horses were used to being staked out, what reason there had been for building a fence around a school that stood out on open prairie, unless it was, perchance, that the Texans thought they ought to have a corral to herd the children in.

While she was thus going on, there came from the corral a bleat in the awe-inspiring tone of *Fa*, and this was followed by a succession of bleats which reminded her of nothing so much as a child getting its hands on the keyboard of an organ. Steve, as if suddenly admonished of something, rose to his feet, excused himself, and disappeared in the direction of the corral.

With the place before her temporarily vacant, and unable to see out of her circle of light except by looking upward, Janet instinctively lifted her eyes to the scene above. Thousands and thousands of stars made the night big and beautiful. They were so clear and so lively, as if they took joy in their shining. A mild southern breeze gave the night motion and perfume. Janet took a deep breath which was hardly a sigh; it

Charles D. Stewart

was rather a big drink of air and the final suspiration of all her worries. As she took in more deeply the constellated heavens and the free fresh spirit of the roaming air, she began to feel that she would rather like to be a sheep-herder herself. From looking at so many, her mind turned back to her selected star, the "captain jewel" of them all, and her eye sought its whereabouts again. In others she could see tremulous tinges of red and blue; but this seemed to be the pure spirit of light. Unconsciously she had put her arm around the dog, as if to hold on to this earth, and Shep, whose affection had been steadily growing, nudged up closer and gave her a sense of warm companionship.

When Steve returned from his mysterious errand, he looked at her a moment and then fetched an armful of wood. The fire, to serve better the purposes of cooking, had been allowed to burn down to coals, and the smouldering embers now gave so little light that the face and figure of his guest were losing themselves in obscurity. As this state of affairs hardly suited him, he piled on the dry mesquite brush and fanned it with his hat into leaping flames. When Janet was lit up to his satisfaction, he put down the hat and resumed his earthen lounge.

As he stretched himself out before her, lithe-limbed and big-chested, the atmosphere of that firelit place seemed filled with a sense of safety. His deliberate manner of speech, quite different from the slowness of a drawl, was the natural voice of that big starry world so generous of time. Occasionally he made a remark which ought to have been flattery, but which, coming from him, was so quiet and true that one might float on it to topics of unknown depth. He was so evidently interested in everything she said, and his attention was so single-minded and sincere, that Janet was soon chatting again upon the subject of her recent circumnavigation of the prairie, which, as she now saw it in the light of the present, seemed more and more a sea of flowers—as the Past always does. Indeed, the whole recent course of her experience was such a novelty—the trip to Texas was her first real adventure in the world—that she saw things with the new vision of a traveler; and the present situation, turning out so happily, put the cap-sheaf on that dream which is truly Life. Janet, recently delivered from all danger, and yet sitting right in the middle of her adventures, had a double advantage; she was living in the present as well as the past, breathing the sweetness of the air, looking up at the big flock of stars and seeing in them all nothing less than the divine shepherding.

"But, of all the wonderful things I ever saw," she exclaimed. "Why, it was worth walking all day to see it."

"What was it?" he asked.

"Sensitive plants. And when I came they all lowered their branches to their sides like—well, slowly, like this—"

She held her right arm out straight and lowered it slowly and steadily to her side. And a most graceful and shapely arm it was.

"I wouldn't have been so much surprised," she continued, "to just see leaves fold together, like clover. You know clover leaves all shut up at night and go to sleep. But these plants were quite large and they actually *moved*. And of course the leaves shut together, too; they were long like little tender locust leaves, and each one folded itself right in the middle."

She placed her hands edge to edge and closed them together to show him.

"But, you know, while they were doing that, they were folding back against their long stems, and the stems were folding back against the branches, and the straight branches were all folding downwards against the main stalk. What I mean is that everything worked together, like this—"

Janet extended both arms with her fingers widely spread; then, as her arms gradually lowered, her fingers closed together.

"It was something like that," she added, "but not exactly; it was ten times as much—something like the ribs of an umbrella going down all around, with stems and rows of locust leaves all along them closing together. And every little leaf was like a rabbit laying back its ears."

"Yes; I know what you mean," said Steve. "They are a kind of mimosa. Some people call them that."

"Well," said Janet, "I sat and watched one. I just touched it with a hatpin and it did that. A person would almost think it had intelligence. And after a while—when it thought I was gone, I suppose—it began to open its leaves and stems and put its arms out again."

She raised her arms slowly, spreading her fingers. Steve was a most attentive listener and spectator. He rather wished there were other plants to imitate.

"But that wasn't really what I started to tell about," she went on. "As I was walking along I came to a—well, you might say a whole *crowd* of them. There was quite a growth like a patch of ferns. I hadn't got to them yet, or even taken particular notice of them,—I must have been ten or twelve feet away,—when they all began to close up. I stopped perfectly still; and pretty soon the green leaves were gone and the place was all changed. Now, how do you suppose those plants ever *knew* I was coming? I would give anything to know how such things can be."

"How much would you give?" inquired Steve.

For a moment, the spirit of this question hung in the balance. He felt the spell of her inquiring eyes as her hand dropped idly on Shep's back.

"Why—do you know?" she asked doubtfully.

"I think I do," he answered. "You see, that kind of plants have very long roots; they run away out. You stepped on their toes."

"Well, I declare," said Janet, enthusiastic again. "And what a way of saying it."

"It looks simple enough, doesn't it?" he remarked.

"And I never thought of it. Why, it was enough to make a person superstitious. Isn't nature wonderful!"

As she took up the coffee, too long neglected, Steve got an imaginary taste of it, and finding it neither hot nor cold, he arose and took her cup. Having refilled it and offered her more of the beans, which to his surprise and gratification she accepted, he made another trip to the corral. In a little while he returned and promptly took his place.

"You were saying this morning," he began, "that you were going to the county-seat. Were you sure that you could find your way all alone?"

"Oh, yes," answered Janet. "I was there before. You see, I took an examination a couple of months ago, when I first came."

"Oh; that's it. What sort of a certificate did that little—examiner—give you?"

There was something in the sound of this question which conveyed to her that he regarded her standing in an examination largely as a matter of luck. Janet felt an instant approval of this philosophy of the matter.

"Third-class," she answered.

"Well, that's better than fourth-class," he remarked.

"Oh—but there *is* no fourth-class," exclaimed Janet.

Her eyes widened as she waited to hear what his reply to this might be.

He entirely ignored the matter.

"That examiner is a kind of a cocky little rooster, isn't he?" he commented.

"Did you ever have any trouble with him?" inquired Janet.

"Me!" He was evidently surprised that she should think so. "Why, no. I don't know him. I just saw him a few times. He is a sort of a dried-up little party. You know I get up to the court-house once in a while to have a brand registered or something like that."

"He *is* rather important—for his size," mused Janet. "And very particular about his looks."

"They have a man teacher at a school near my house," remarked Steve, in no seeming connection.

"I suppose he has a first-class certificate," said Janet. "Until lately it was easy to get a school in Texas. But the country school boards rate you by your certificate more and more. This time I am going to get first-class, or at least second. If I don't I'll have to go back North."

"What kind of questions does that fellow ask when he examines people?" Steve inquired.

"Well—for instance—'Give the source and course of the Orizaba.'"

"Huh!" remarked Steve.

"To tell the truth," said Janet, "I wouldn't have got even third-class if it hadn't been for the way I pulled through in geography."

"Are you good in geography?"

"Hardly. I just passed. He asked a great many questions about climate, and every time he asked that I wrote that it was salubrious. You see," she explained, with a sly little air, "in the children's geographies the climate of a country is nearly always salubrious. So I took a chance on every country. That brought my average up."

"Good for you," exclaimed Steve. "Nothing like beating them at their own game. Won't you have some more coffee?"

"No, thank you," said Janet. "Two cups is really more than I ought to drink at night."

Having risen in expectation of getting the coffee, he gave the fire another armful of mesquite.

"You take a good deal of notice of flowers, don't you!" he said, sitting down again.

"A person could hardly help it in Texas. Lilies and trumpet-flowers and lobelias and asters and dahlias and wax-plants—they all grow wild here. And in spring it is just wonderful. There is scarcely room for grass."

"Texas won't be like that long, if it keeps on."

"No?"

"These plants all grow from seed. And when the land is heavily grazed they don't have a chance to plant themselves. They become—what do you call it—extinguished?"

"Extinct," prompted Janet.

"On my ranch, about twelve miles from here, it isn't what it used to be in springtime. We've got it pretty heavily stocked; we're working it over into shorthorn. This place that we're on now has a fence all around it; the country is becoming crowded. And they are breaking farms all the time, too. It won't last long."

"Won't that be a shame!" said Janet. "People spoil everything, don't they? I am glad I came down here just to see the Texas prairie in spring. Even if I do have to go back again. Just look at that!"

She reached out, and, grasping a handful, she bent the still rooted bouquet so that the light shone full upon its countenance.

"How did you come to know the names of them all?" he asked.

"Why, we grow them in gardens up North. I know their names in that way. They are old acquaintances."

"Oh, that's it. Well, it isn't hard to grow them here. Us fellows out on the prairie make all our flower-beds round."

Janet paused.

"Oh!" she exclaimed. "You mean the *horizon*. Isn't that an idea! I am going to tell that to Ruth Ferguson the first time I write."

Steve made no reply. Janet gave her attention for a space to the beans. Then, suddenly reminded, she put down her fork.

"Mr. Brown! If you were teaching just ten or twelve children, wouldn't it strike you as rather foolish to call the roll every morning? You know there were only fourteen pupils in the school where I was substituting; so of course I got acquainted with them all right away. Well, one morning when the weather was bad there were only six present; so when the hour came I just began to teach. But a little boy who is in the first reader held up his hand and told me I had to call the roll first. I could hardly keep from smiling. As if I couldn't see the six that were there. Then I made inquiry and I found that Miss Porter called the roll when there were only four there. Doesn't it seem funny for a person to go through a formality like that just because—well, just because?"

"That's because you've got sense," said Steve.

She dropped her eyes and ate. When this remark had had time to pass over, Janet's sociable spirit, never self-conscious for long, began to unfold its leaves and raise its stems and lift up its branches again.

In this juncture, the dog profited. Shep had been giving her such unremitting attention, his wistful brown eyes following each forkful as it went from plate to mouth, that Janet's consciousness of her selfish situation kept bearing in upon her till now every bean carried reproach with it. Thinking to convince him that it was only beans, and not desirable, she put him down a forkful from her own too generous allowance. She was surprised at the suddenness with which it disappeared. Beans were his staff of life also, a discovery which made her smile. And as one good turn deserves another—at least Shep seemed to think so—she was expected to do it again; thus supper, with his assistance, was soon over. And now Janet, with nothing whatever to do, sat face to face with her situation.

"Have you got a dishpan?" she inquired.

"Oh, you don't need to mind that. I haven't got anything you are used to. I just take them down to the stream and swab them off with a bunch of dry grass."

"Oh!" remarked Janet.

She felt, however, that it would be easier to be doing something. She gathered things together and made general unrest among the dishes. Mr. Brown, instead of being stirred by this operation of cleaning up, stretched himself out more contentedly, moved up a little closer, and took still fuller possession of her presence; and as he did so he poked up the fire and struck her a light on a new topic. But this time the train of conversation did not catch. Janet was thinking. And like most of us she could not talk well while thinking.

Mr. Brown seemed quite contented, then, with silence and peace. Evidently he too was thinking. After a little time he sat up and reached into an inside pocket. He drew forth a large leather wallet which, upon being opened, disclosed two compartments well filled with bank-notes and documentary-looking papers. There was another compartment with a flap on it and a separate fastening, opening which he took out an object wrapped in tissue paper. Having carefully unwrapped it, he folded the paper again and placed it where it would not blow away.

"That's my mother's picture," he said, handing it over formally to his guest.

Janet received it rather vaguely and sat looking at it, saying nothing.

"She died just last winter," he added, in his usual deliberate way.

"Oh, did she?"

What else to say, she hardly knew. Turning it to the light she studied it more closely and noted each resemblance to his own features, looking up at him in an impersonal sort of way and with a soberness of countenance which was a reflection of his own entirely serious mood.

"She had a very kind-looking face," she said.

To this there was no reply. Janet, about to hand it back, was momentarily in doubt as to how long a proper respect should prompt her to retain it; this, however, settled itself when she observed that he had ready to offer her a long newspaper clipping.

"I had the editor put some of that in myself," he said, reaching the long ribbon of paper over to her.

It was an obituary of Mrs. Stephen P. Brown, who passed to "the realms beyond" on the eighteenth of November. With this Janet found no difficulty.

"But," he added suddenly as it occurred to him, "I didn't have him print that part at the bottom. He just put that in himself. I mean that stuff about me."

Janet at once turned her attention to the bottom. He sat silently with the wallet in hand, his countenance a shade more solemn than usual. In the midst of this waiting there came a wail from the corral and he left suddenly upon one of his unexplained errands, this time without excusing himself. He got back while Janet was still engaged upon the article. When she looked up he was standing beside the fire looking down at her. There was something new in his face, a look half lugubrious, semi-humorous, apologetic.

"We've got another lamb," he announced.

"Oh!—another little lamb?" she exclaimed.

"There are only three so far. Three lambs and two mothers. It hasn't really got started yet, but I'm afraid it will. My herder ought to have got back yesterday and brought help along."

"Then you have a great deal to do?" queried Janet.

"Yes; after it once gets really started. Then it never rains but it pours. I have been hoping it would hold off a day or two longer; but you can't tell exactly."

He put more wood on the fire and took his place again.

"You mustn't let me interfere with your work," she suggested.

"Oh, that isn't it at all. I was just explaining. I'll get through somehow; it won't amount to anything."

With a characteristic sweep of his arm he waved the whole subject aside as if he did not want to have it interfere with her reading of the newspaper clipping. Janet had dropped it absent-mindedly in her lap; she now took it up again. Besides the tribute to Mrs. Brown's character, who was not a native of Texas but had come to the state in her girlhood from West Virginia, there was a considerable memoir of Stephen Brown, senior, relating his activities and adventures as a Texas patriot. He had "crossed the Great Divide" six years before. Finally, there was a paragraph of sympathy with the only son, "one of our most valued citizens."

"Your father knew Houston, didn't he?" remarked Janet.

"Oh, yes; he knew a lot about him."

"How interesting that must have been. Your father was a pioneer, wasn't he?"

"Oh, no. You've got to go back pretty far in history to be a Texas pioneer. He was just a Texan."

She gave another perusal to certain parts and offered it back.

"There is another piece on the other side," he said.

She turned it over and found a shorter clipping carefully pasted to the back. This also she read.

AN ARTISTIC MONUMENT

Mr. Stephen Brown yesterday received from Austin the monument which he had made for the grave of his mother,

Mrs. Stephen P. Brown, who died last November. It is a most beautiful work of art and was much admired by those who saw it. It is a massive block of imported gray granite skillfully carved with clusters of grapes in high relief. Mr. Brown ordered it from the leading marble-cutters in Austin. The reverse side of the stone was cut after his own design, and consists simply of a Lone Star. On the base is the word Mother. Many of our citizens were enabled to inspect it as it went up Main Street, Mr. Jonas Hicks stopping his three yoke of oxen to accommodate those who wished to look it over. It will be by far the most beautiful work of art in our local cemetery.

Janet folded up the clipping carefully, according to the creases in it, and passed it back. When he had returned it to its compartment in the wallet,—an operation which was somewhat delayed by his difficulties with the tissue paper around the picture,—she questioned him further about the Comanche Indians and his father's adventures in the war with Mexico. Now the conversational situation was turned about, Janet becoming the interlocutor; and as she had the advantage of so copious a source of information, there was no end to her questioning. And as the stream of talk broadened, it began to include his own experiences and adventures, most interesting of which, to Janet, was a short account of the fight of a sheriff's posse with the train-robbers intrenched near the Post Oaks, a most determined encounter in which the sheriff was among those killed while Steve Brown received only a blunted thumb, for the clumsy appearance of which his story was rather an apology.

"That's all I got," he said. "And it works as good as ever."

To demonstrate which fact, he held it up and made it work.

Now that she had material by which to lead the conversation, she found him not nearly so taciturn as she had at first thought him. Indeed, he talked on without remembering to fix the fire. And when it had nearly faded out he continued on, unconscious of the fact that the real Janet was no longer in sight except as she was partially lit by the moon which now hove upon the scene.

"But I am keeping you up too late," she said, suddenly rising.

Steve gathered himself together and stood up, hat in hand.

"Oh, I am used to all hours," he said. "Anyway, I've got to keep an eye on things."

"And I am sorry to put you out," she added.

"Don't mention it. I put myself out. I could let you have a lantern if you need it. There's a piece of candle and some matches on the top bunk. It's down near the foot."

"Oh, that will be all the light I need. Good-night."

"Good-night, Miss Janet,"—saluting her by raising his hat to the side of his head and then bringing it down with a large sweep.

When the door had closed upon her and the shack showed light at all its cracks, he turned and went to the corral, closely followed by Shep. He took a look at the two sheep, each confined in one of the narrow little prison-pens along with the lamb whose property it was. The lambs were evidently full of milk; they were sleeping. Seeing that all was well, he got an old discarded saddle out of the shed, threw it on his shoulder, and descended to the general level to find himself a buffalo-wallow. Having picked one out he kicked a longhorn skull away from its vicinity, threw the saddle down at its edge, and lined the grassy interior with his slicker. Then he sat down in the middle, crushing the slicker deep into the spring bloom. Here he sat a while.

It is not easy for the human mind, constituted as it is, to pick out a bed on a prairie. It offers such a large field of choice, and no grounds for preference. Steve had long ago formed the habit of sleeping in a wallow, always to be found within a short distance, and, when found, possessing the advantage of being a "place." Such a place—a bowl-like depression—was made by the bison who pawed away the tough sward to get at mother earth, and then wore it deep and circular as he tried to roll on his unwieldy hump. Steve Brown, anywhere between Texas and Montana, had often slept in the "same old place," though in a different locality, and for some reason he was never so content—either because it was really a "place," or because he liked a bed that sagged in the middle, or because (which is more likely) he found a certain atmosphere of sleep in one of these places so long ago dedicated to rest and comfort. Which hollow is all that is now left of the buffalo—a vacancy.

He sat down in the middle, his attention fixed upon the shack, which now existed as a sort of picture of itself drawn in lines of light. When suddenly it was erased from the night, he pressed the slicker down and lay back with his head in the saddle. He folded his hands and waited, looking straight up. In a little while the world receded and he was only conscious of sundry stars. Thus, looking heaven in the eye, his hands clasped across his chest, Steve Brown sunk to sleep, his head and feet sticking up at the ends. Again Eternity held sway; and only Shep was left.

Shep turned round and round till he had trampled a place among the flowers, his usual way of winding up the day. He lay down in it with his chin on his paws. But soon he got up and went at it again. He milled round and round, with several pauses as if he were not quite satisfied; then he dropped down with a decisiveness that settled the matter for good. With his chin on the brink of the wallow he went to sleep; or rather he went as near asleep as a dog with such great responsibilities allows himself to do.

CHAPTER VIII

The sheep, having several times broken the silence of the dawn, were growing impatient to be let out. Now that the sun had appeared and the bars were not let down, there was unanimous expression of opinion in the corral, an old wether stamping his foot sternly and leading the chorus with a doleful note. It was very much as if he had put the question and they had all voted "aye." What was the matter with the man who was running this part of the world?

Steve Brown was otherwise engaged. He was sitting on the ground behind the storm-shed with a lamb in his lap. He was trying to remove from its back the pelt of another lamb which had been neatly fitted on over its own. This was a trick on the mother of the dead lamb intended to get her to care for the present lamb, who was an orphan; which is to say, the extra pelt was the lamb's meal-ticket, and she had given him several meals on the evidence of smell. The deception had worked all the more readily because she had not had time to become familiar with her own lamb's voice; and now that a sort of vocal relationship had been established between the two, things promised to go along naturally, with probably a little insistence upon the lamb's part.

In accordance with the usual practice in such cases, the pelt, with head and legs removed, had been fastened on by means of holes cut at the corners, through which the live one's legs were inserted, care being taken to leave on the tail, which part, when a lamb is nursing, is most convenient to smell.

As Steve Brown was not used to this sort of tailoring, he had made rather too close a fit of it, and now that it was dried up at the edges and slightly shrunk, he found difficulty in removing it. Seeing, upon further effort, that he could not get it off without risk of straining the lamb's anatomy, he laid the problem across his knees again and searched his pockets for his knife. He had felt for it, not very thoroughly, before. The knife seemed to be lost.

Janet, awakened by the clamor in the pen, arose from the bunk and set to work arranging her hair. Rather drowsily she moved about through the rifts of sunshine which beamed from the cracks; then, as she realized what a golden day the sun was weaving, she put her eye to a crack and looked out. In her elongated picture of things there were several miles of prairie, the sun just edge-to-edge with the horizon, and any amount of blue sky above. In the sky were some birds soaring at a great height. Smaller birds went skimming over the prairie,—now a golden meadowlark, then a darker scissortail snipping the air off behind it in swift flight. Suddenly, and rather precipitately, there came from around the corner of the storm-shed a lamb in full action. Its gait was as effective as it was erratic; it looked very much as if the legs were running away with it.

From the corner of the shed it made a joyous gambol in the direction of the fire and the steaming kettle, from which point it made for the down-slope of the knoll. Steve Brown, whose legs were none too long for the race, came running after. A moment later the dog arrived on the scene; he made a sudden dash and performed his part in a most creditable manner, overtaking the lamb and upsetting it with a poke of his nose. The lamb, not at all disconcerted by the tumble, which was only a variation of its method of progress, came over on its knees and rose at once to go ahead; but the delay had been sufficient. Steve caught up; and the next instant, the truant, feeling the ground removed from under it, hung helpless across the hand of its captor.

"Je-e-emima!" Steve remarked. "You're feeling awful glad this morning."

Janet, who could not see the end of this performance, but only that part of it which came within range of the crack, stepped back in surprise. As who would not be surprised to see a black lamb with a white head and white legs, and two tails. Such being the result of her prying upon the world, she turned her attention to her toilet again and made haste to go out and see whether her eyes had deceived her.

In the mean time Steve, not being able to find the knife, stood with the lamb in his arms and bent the whole force of his mind upon the problem of its whereabouts. Suddenly he remembered that he had last used it in front of the shack to put the pelt on the lamb. Naturally, it was still there. Having it again, he sat down near the fire-hole, where he could keep an eye on the kettle, placed the lamb on his lap and opened the blade. He had just got to work on one of the legs when the door opened and his guest made her appearance. He rose at once to pay his respects, the lamb in one hand and his hat in the other.

"Good-morning, Miss Janet."

"Good-morning, Mr. Brown. It is a very beautiful day, isn't it?"

"First-class," he replied. "I'm just doing a little work on this lamb. I guess you know him; he's the one you saw when you first came."

"What! The one that stepped in the sugar bowl?"

"Yes, that's him. He doesn't look exactly natural, does he? I had to make some changes in him. You see his mother didn't think she wanted any lamb. But another sheep had one that died and I could see she wanted a lamb, so that was an opening for this fellow. And I had to fix him up so that she'd take him."

"What a funny thing to do," said Janet.

"Isn't it! Do you wonder that sheep-herders go crazy? Just wait a minute, Miss Janet, and I'll have this off of him."

He sat down again with the lamb in his lap. Turning it over on its back he set to work on the hind legs. Janet, becoming interested, stooped down beside him. She patted the infant on its high forehead.

"And didn't the other sheep want to adopt him?" she asked.

"Oh, no. Sheep don't believe in charity."

"And won't even have their own sometimes! Isn't that strange!"

"Some of them seem to be built that way, especially if it is their first one. But that sheep didn't have much milk anyway, and maybe she thought he might as well die. If it hadn't been for that I would have tried to make her take him. But I saw the other sheep could do better by him."

Charles D. Stewart

"There is really a great deal to think of, isn't there?" said Janet, lending a hand to the operation by catching hold of a too active hind leg. "But I don't see how you could fool her that way. Couldn't she see that this lamb had a white head? And white legs? And an extra tail?"

"Oh, they don't go by looks," he explained. "They go by smell. And later on by voice, too. Appearances don't count."

"The idea! You seem to know all about them."

"Not much," he said. "I'm no sheep-man."

"But anyway, you do get along with them."

"If they were my sheep," he answered, "and I wasn't responsible for them, I wouldn't be so particular. Especially with this one; he has been a lot of trouble. As far as money goes—he isn't worth over fifty cents—I would have let him die."

"Oh, no-o-o-o!" protested Janet, lending further assistance with the pelt.

"But after I had carried him around with me all day I got to feeling responsible for him."

"A person naturally would," said Janet.

"And besides," he added, holding the lamb upright while she, with her more skillful fingers, removed the fore legs from the armholes of the pelt, "a fellow sort of hates to lose the first one, you know."

Janet, finding the lambskin left on her hands, examined it curiously, running her fingers over the soft black wool.

"What shall I do with this, Mr. Brown?"

"Oh, just throw it away. But no," he added, upon second thought, "I guess you had better keep that. It would be good for you to sit on."

Following this suggestion she took it to her "place" on the prairie and spread it down. Then, as he seemed to be waiting for her, she returned.

"Miss Janet, I guess you'll want to wash up. The best I can offer you is the place down below the spring. You'll find some soap down there in a cigar-box. The bank is a little steep for you to climb down, so I guess you had better go round and get in the front way. On your way around you'll find a towel on a bush; it is pretty clean,—I washed it last night. And you'd better take the lambskin along to kneel on."

Steve carried the lamb away to its breakfast. Janet took the pelt and followed his instructions, going down the slope and skirting round the base of the knoll till she came to where the stream issued forth.

The little gully was hardly more than a deep grass-grown ditch made by the spring as it won its way out of the heart of the knoll; or rather it was a green hallway, overtopped with a frieze of mesquite, leading in privately to the source of the stream. Janet, as she entered the house-like cosiness of this diminutive valley, felt very much as if she had just stepped in out of the universe. On a prairie there is such an insistent stare of space, so great a lack of stopping-place for the mind, that this little piece of outdoors, with the sun shining in at its eastern end, was a veritable snug-harbor in an ocean of land. As she turned and looked out of its sunny portal, she told herself that if she had to live in the shack this place would be her front yard.

Charles D. Stewart

Just below the spring was a grassy bank against which the water ran invitingly; she spread the lambskin here, rolled up her sleeves, took off her collar, and conformed to the customs of the place. The cool water was so invigorating, and there was something so intimate in the live push of the current against her hand, that she lathered her arms an unnecessary number of times and kept rinsing them off. It was a brisk little stream and so bent upon its business that she could almost feel its impatience when she obstructed it,—for which reason, probably, she interfered with it the more; and finally, being done, she made a little heap of foam in her palm and reached it down just to see the water run away with it.

As she came round to the sheep-path again, she met Steve, who had been standing on the side of the knoll and started down the moment he saw her. Evidently he had been waiting his turn.

"Breakfast is all ready," he announced as he passed. "I'll be up in a minute."

By the time she reached the shack there was a great spluttering and splashing and blowing of water down below. It was Mr. Brown "washing up." In little more than the minute he was back again. Finding her seated upon the lambskin, he took his place opposite her and passed the hot bread.

"I saw you chasing that lamb this morning," she said, quite directly. "I was looking out of a crack to find what the weather was like."

"Did you? Did you see the dog throw him?"

"No; I couldn't see it all. But I saw how he had learned to use his legs. Why, it doesn't seem possible."

"Oh, that's nothing. He's an old hand now—this is his third day on earth."

"Yes; but isn't he unusually smart?"

"Oh, no. They've got to catch on pretty quick, you know, or they couldn't keep up with the procession. He's just about like the rest of them. They all learn fast."

"But it hardly seems possible that such a *helpless* little thing as he was could learn so much. Why, when I first saw him he was just able to stand up."

"They're animals," replied Steve, spreading a thick coat of molasses on a large piece of hot bread. "It only takes them a few minutes to learn standing up?"

"But they do have to learn, don't they?"

"Oh, yes. They don't always get it right the first time. Lambs make mistakes the same as anybody else. But if they get started out right, with a good meal the first thing, and a warm sleep, they go ahead surprisingly. The trouble with them at first is that they are a little weak."

"I don't suppose, then, that a lamb can get right up and follow the flock?" she queried.

"Oh, no. That would be expecting too much. They can toddle around pretty well in a few hours; but they couldn't really travel till they've had time to grow strong."

Janet paused in her questioning. She spent a few moments reflecting upon the information gained thus far.

"Then I can't understand, Mr. Brown, how you can herd those sheep and take care of the lambs too. You surely can't carry them all?"

"That's just what the trouble is," he answered. "I guess that Harding must be drunk. If he doesn't get back soon and bring help it's likely to get serious."

"And what will you do?"

"You see, Miss Janet," he said, laying down knife and fork for a formal statement of the difficulty, "when you're grazing a bunch of sheep and one of them drops a lamb she stays right there with it. That is, she does if she is one of the natural kind. Pretty soon the flock has gone on and she is left behind. After a while another has a lamb and she drops out and is left behind. And so on. So there ought to be somebody to take them back to the corral. But of course the lambs can't travel. They've got to be carried."

"How long do you suppose that man will take—at the farthest?"

"He ought to be back now. He may come any time. If I only knew he was coming before night I would know how to manage. I would go right along and leave the wet-lambs and their mothers stringing along behind; then when he came with help he could get them in for the night. They would be all right to stay out on the prairie for a while—all except those whose mothers didn't care for them. But I would do that; and those whose mothers didn't stick to them would have to die."

"Oh, that would be such a shame!" Janet's eyes opened wide as she contemplated this state of affairs. "And how about the ones who had mothers? Would it be all right if they had to stay out on the prairie till the next day?"

"No-o-o-o—it would hardly do to leave lambs scattered around on the prairie all night even if their mothers were with them. Coyotes would get them."

"Oh, dear! Don't you think, Mr. Brown, that that man is quite certain to get back sometime to-day?"

"I don't see how he can stay away much longer. He knows mighty well he has my horse, too. He might come along any time."

For a while they ate in silence.

"Miss Janet," he said suddenly, "I don't think you had better start out alone again. When he gets back with my horse and I am free of this place, I can show you the road and see that you are all right. I would feel more satisfied that way."

"Well, then, couldn't I be of some assistance—if I stay?"

"Oh, that isn't necessary. I'll get along somehow. I don't suppose, though, that you'd care to sit here alone at the shack; so maybe you'd better come along with me. And if you want to drop behind once in a while and help a lamb out, why, of course you can. You seem to be pretty handy with them."

This plan was adopted. When breakfast was over he let down the bars; the sheep poured forth; Shep sprang to life and barked orders right and left. The crowding multitude spread out on the prairie in grazing order, and when Shep had executed certain commands necessary to get them headed in the right direction, the trio of caretakers began their slow progress through the day. Shep, subject to orders, followed at

Steve's heels; Janet walked at his right hand; thus they wandered along in the desultory manner of the sheep-herder, standing a while, sitting down a while, advancing now and then as the flock grazed farther away.

"There's number one," Steve remarked casually.

They had ascended, almost imperceptibly, one of those slow rises or folds in the prairie from which more distant objects, if there are any, come into view. Janet had just been taking her bearings; ahead of them there had now come to sight the long file of trees which marked the course of Comanche Creek; looking back she could still see the shack, quite plainly, on its knoll. As he spoke, and pointed, her eyes followed the new direction, off to the left. A sheep had fallen out of the flock; she was now standing some distance behind. From the way she nosed in the grass without advancing, it was evident what had taken place.

"Well, good-bye," said Janet. Then, feeling suddenly that these words had too serious a sound, she added, "But I suppose I will catch up with you before long."

"Shall I go over with you?"

"Oh, no," she answered, and hurried away.

"Don't forget what I said about the creek," he called out after her.

As she looked back he pointed first at the shack and then at the creek, bringing his arm around in a semicircle as if it were a sort of dial-hand to the prairie. "Don't get lost," he added.

When she nodded to show that she understood, he strode on

after the sheep. They had been gaining ground steadily and had got far ahead.

Janet, reaching the scene of the nativity, became very much interested. The lamb was just beginning to look up and take notice; she stooped over him in rapt contemplation. His little merino back was wrinkled as fine as a frown. His little hoofs were already beginning to feel the ground under them; he was going to rise! Then ensued a lamb's usual drunken contest with the laws of gravity. While he stepped on air and tried to get the hang of things, Janet followed his fortunes with bated breath. When he had got his four legs firmly planted, the first thing he did was to shake himself; and he did it with such vigor that he upset himself. This was a surprise to Janet if not to the lamb; he had shaken himself off his feet; everything had to be done over again. He seemed a little stultified by this turn of affairs; but though he was down the fall had not knocked any of the ambition out of him; he immediately went at it again. This time he conquered and stood right up to the bar of life, much to Janet's relief.

Having filled himself and spent a moment looking at nothing in particular, he decided that the best thing to do was to veer around and have some more; in taking this step, however, there was some sort of error in the proceedings and he went down forward on his knees. A moment later the hind legs stumbled and fell, and he was all down; now he decided to take a rest. As the mother nosed him over and showed every sign of affection, Janet began to see that her services were not needed; her presence was of no consequence whatever. There was nothing for her to do but to stroke his back and pat him on the head; having done which she rose and again went forward upon her charitable mission.

The flock by this time had eaten its way into the distance. It was not so far away, however, but that she could soon have

Charles D. Stewart

overtaken it. She walked along at a moderate pace, looking alternately to right and left for such as might fall under her care.

She had not gone far when she sighted another. As this one had dropped out of the right wing of the army ahead, he was off to one side of her present course. By the time she arrived he had already succeeded in standing up; he even took a distinct step; then he shook himself like a dog just out of water. Like the other lamb, he shook himself down; he hit the ground with rather more decisive a drop. When he had again mastered the difficulties, and achieved his reward, Janet sat down near by and waited to see whether the two would become acquainted. This again proved to be a happy union.

Janet felt a little disappointed. She had expected to be of some use. Now that she had proved to be a mere looker-on she began to take thought about the lamb's future. There came to her again those words—"The coyotes would get them." She rose at once. A man would carry them back to the corral; why not she? She took the lamb in her arms intending to go off a distance and see whether the mother would follow. The experiment proved unnecessary, however; the ewe not only followed but kept close at her side. Accompanied thus by the mother she went back to the first halting-place where the other ewe joined them; thence she set a course straight for the shack, a lamb on each arm and a sheep at each side of her. Things went much easier than she had expected.

In this turn of affairs, she felt quite satisfied. Although it was the first time she had ever touched a lamb or had any experience with a sheep, the work seemed perfectly natural. Indeed, as she marched along between the two watchful ewes, and hugged to her breast the warm objects of their attention, it seemed to her—a very puzzling delusion—that she had done this same thing before; it was like a half-faded memory. Nor did it seem natural to think of Mr. Brown as a stranger; it seemed that she had known him a long time ago—always. Possibly this was because she felt so much at home in this sort of work. Then, too, we dream dreams, and they have a way of bringing themselves to pass in some shape or other.

Having reached the corral she managed to let down the bars without getting the infants mixed up—a matter which had given her much concern; and now that she had them safely inside she thought it advisable to wait a while and make sure that family relations were going to be permanent, after her interference. She rested herself by sitting on the top rail of the corral; meantime she took an interested survey of the stuffed clothes of Mr. Pete Harding under whose manly presentment the lambs enjoyed protection. Mr. Brown had made a very good imitation of a man by filling the herder's working-clothes with marsh grass; the figure had been made to stand up by means of a pole thrust through the fence, to the end of which Mr. Harding was suspended by the neck as if he had been hung in effigy. The man himself had not yet put in his appearance. Janet, as she thought of him, scanned the horizon for signs of his approach. There was no indication of his coming. But still the day was not half over; possibly, she told herself, he would arrive early in the afternoon. Having become satisfied that all was well, so far as the lambs were concerned, she put up the top bar and went forth again to her work.

By looking back occasionally and sighting her route by means of the shack and the storm-shed, the relative positions of which she had been careful to observe when she first went out, she held her course so well that when she next came in sight of the line of trees she was at the same point as before.

Charles D. Stewart

Here she set straight out for the bend in the creek, which landmark was to guide her on the next stage of her quest. As before, she kept a sharp lookout for stranded sheep.

She had not gone a great distance when another case presented itself. This time it was twins. The pair were sleeping. The mother, having licked them nicely into shape, had lain down beside them; when Janet arrived she got up suddenly and stared at her in alarm. The twins had evidently been successful, so far, in all their undertakings, not the least of which is to take a rest. They were in very good condition to be carried. She took them up and arranged them comfortably, one on each arm, and soon they were on their way to safety, the anxious mother trotting first to one side of Janet and then to the other. These also were added to the ones in the corral.

Janet did not feel so tired but that she could have turned about at once; she would have done so had it not been that it was dinner-time and she was hungry. Mr. Brown had taken along with him an extra large lunch which he expected her to share with him somewhere along the shaded banks of the Comanche; the little plan passed momentarily through her mind as she raised the lid of the box and took out a pan of beans. There was also a piece of bread left; it tasted better than she would have expected cold hot-bread to do.

Luckily for the work she had taken upon herself, Steve Brown had planned a route for the day which any one could easily follow. He was going to graze the sheep along Comanche Creek, downstream, on the right-hand side; he would bring them back not very wide of the same course. This arrangement he had made entirely with a view to being quickly found in case help arrived; he had left a note behind giving instructions. As this was all very plain sailing, Janet saw that she would be quite free to come and go, and she had been quick to turn this arrangement to the lambs' advantage. When she had satisfied the worst of her hunger she started out again. The consciousness that she could find him whenever she wished, and was, virtually, in touch with him all the time, made her task entirely enjoyable.

This time she reached the creek and gave herself over to its guidance. Comanche Creek, like other prairie streams, had its line of trees which very plainly belonged to it and not to the prairie. This impression of foreignness to the region was emphasized by their extending in unbroken procession from horizon to horizon, as if they were merely crossing the plains. While the stream hurried on to its congregation of waters, the trees seemed bound for some distant forest. Quite strictly they kept to the course; none of them, beech, hickory, live-oak, nor pecan, encroached beyond the right of way nor seemed ever to have been forgetful that these were the Plains. It was very much as if they recognized that trees ought not to grow here. As, indeed, they ought not. The prairie is itself as much as is the ocean or forest, and it has no room to spare. Space, like wood and water, must have its own exclusive regions wherein to exercise its larger and deeper spell. These were the earthly fastnesses of space; and so preempted. Many grapevines looped along the route, some of them of ancient growth, hanging like big ropes from tree to tree; these had the appearance of keeping a still closer regard to the direction of the stream itself, their more sinuous wood flowing along in a like spirit and keeping the waters company. Nowhere so artfully, perhaps, as in a prairie stream, are eye and ear addressed by the manifold activities of wood and water. To come across it in the course of a long monotonous journey is as sudden as falling in love—and very much like it.

Comanche Creek, having such advantages of contrast and sharp comparison, was well calculated to strike the mind with the whole charm of stream and forest; and so it worked upon Janet. To her right was the prairie as monotonous as duty; to her left the creek with its mirrored vistas, its rippling bends, its comfortable resting-places where sun and shade played together. Inviting as it all was, however, she kept well out on the open where her business lay; only occasionally did she let her gaze wander from its set task to loiter in this more restful scene. She kept on looking for lambs. But after a while she awoke to the fact that she had been walking closer and closer when she ought to be keeping out on the prairie; instead of using it as a guide in her work she was making a companion of it. She turned at once and marched out to the scene of duty.

As she got out nearer to the centre of her field of operations, —twelve hundred sheep cut a pretty wide swath,—she thought she heard the cry of a lamb. She stopped and listened. All was silence. It might have been imagination, assisted, possibly, by some rumor of the distant flock; but yet the still small voice had seemed to come from somewhere near at hand. She went forward, listening intently. Presently she heard it again; then she saw him. He was so close that she could see his little red tongue as he opened his mouth and called to her.

Poor little lamb! There was not a sheep in sight. There was just him and the prairie. He was barely managing to stand up; she could easily see that he was on his last legs as well as his first ones. As she went to him he took a step or two as if to meet her, but his legs lacked stiffening and he fell on his nose. She ran and picked him up. As she took him in her arms he opened his mouth again and called upon his mother.

Which way to take him in search of milk became now a pressing problem. She thought she felt him shiver. If he was to be saved, it would not do for him to starve much longer;

nature demands that if a lamb is to live he must have his first meal without delay. She paused to decide the matter, holding his passive little hoofs in her hand. To keep right on after the flock might prove the quickest way; but again it might not; it would be taking a chance. Back at the corral, far though it was, the services of a mother were certain. The surest way seemed the best to her, and having decided so, she turned about at once, walking rapidly.

The return trip seemed very long, and the forced pace told upon her strength. She kept it up, however, till the goal had been reached. Having her orphan inside the bars she deposited him in a corner while she turned her attention to the row of little stalls or prison-pens which were built along the outside of the fence. This institution she had observed with great interest. Each pen was just large enough to crowd a ewe in, being calculated to allow her no liberty in any way; they were all built so that sheep could be put into them from the inside of the corral. She opened one of them, seized upon the first lamb at hand and put it in, and when the fond mother put her nose in after it Janet gave her a good push from behind and sent her in also; then she abstracted the rightful lamb and put the other in its place. Having closed the opening she climbed over the fence and sat down on the prairie beside the pen where she could look in between the rails and watch developments.

The lamb, probably because it had gone too long without that first drink which is the making of a lamb, did not seem able to rise. Janet put her hand in between the rails and gave it a lift. Once it had its legs under it, it managed for itself. To Janet's great satisfaction it filled up visibly. When it was done, she let out the ewe, who hastened to find her own again, knocking down the orphan in the process of getting out. As he made no effort to rise, Janet again took him in her arms.

The lamb seemed dispirited and chilled. This is a condition which is quite likely to overtake a "wet-lamb" if it is neglected from the outset, in which case its little stock of vitality is not easily regained. Despite the brightness of the weather there was a touch of chill in the air. Janet sat down in the doorway of the shack and held the lamb in her lap, doubling her skirt up over it in order to get it warm. Like any other lamb it submitted to whatever was done to it. Now it lay so quietly in her lap, and looked so innocent and helpless, that she felt permanently responsible for it. Especially as she did not know what else to do with it. Presently she felt it growing warmer and warmer; then it went to sleep.

Janet was tired. She sat there watching the prairie. In the sky the same dark birds were soaring. The suspended effigy of Mr. Pete Harding, swayed by the slightest breeze, moved its loose-hung arms and legs as if it were being visited by the drunken spirit of its owner. At intervals the solitude found expression in a sheep's automatic *baa*. The birds, which were buzzards, wheeled round and round as the time passed and brought them nothing. One of them, tired of wheeling round and round, sat on one of the posts of the corral and waited for something to happen. These were the dusky angels that carried away the lamb's body of the day before; she had seen its little white bones down at the foot of the knoll. The present watcher, a stoop-shouldered, big, rusty-black bird, was quite indifferent to human presence; he sat on his post like a usurer on his high stool, calculating and immovable. Janet knew what was in his mind. She drew the lamb a little closer and tucked her skirt in around it. Again she fell to contemplating the prairie—and the sky. The birds above seemed connected with the machinery of Time. At unexpected moments a sheep gave voice to it all "in syllable of dolour."

No, she would not really want to be a sheepherder; at least

not alone. Last night, or whenever Steve Brown was about, everything looked quite different. Even now, she reflected, it was not so bad as it might be, and she did not really mind it much; it was his place; he was just over the horizon somewhere; and as long as it was his place she did not feel so lonesome. He had long ago turned the flock about; she could picture him as he followed them along, nearer and nearer. After a while he would be home.

She sat holding the lamb till the sun began to redden; then it occurred to her that, under the circumstances, it was her duty to get supper. It was a welcome thought; she would see what she could do. She put the orphan at the foot of the bunk, drew the quilt over it and set to work.

It had now become apparent that she was destined to spend another night at the shack; this, however, gave her no serious concern. It entered her mind only in the form of the pleasant reflection that nobody would be worried by her absence; the farmer's family would think she had gone to the county-seat and then reached her destination at Merrill; the folks at Merrill would think she was still at the school, all of which was very fortunate, and so she thought no more about it. She was mainly concerned with the lambs, and particularly, at the present moment, with supper. She spread down her two white napkins, which had not seen service the night before, placing them corner to corner or diamondwise on the ground; then she set the table and examined further into the resources of the provision box. While the fire was getting itself under way, she completed the effect by arranging some flowers in a cup and placing a nosegay upon the bosom of nature. Before long there was a good bed of coals in the fire-hole.

Supper was just ready when the flock reached the knoll and began streaming up the slope into the corral; then followed Steve Brown escorted by three sheep. He carried four lambs,

Charles D. Stewart

one on each arm, and two others whose heads protruded from the breast of his coat.

"Four more!" she exclaimed, stepping forward to meet them. "Did you get all there were, Mr. Brown?"

"I got all I saw, Miss Janet," he answered, casting a bright and intelligent look at the fire-hole. "And I was afraid I had lost you. You got supper, didn't you? That looks nice."

Steve Brown's conversation was largely illumined by the light of his eye; likewise his silences, which were many. They were direct eyes which paid close attention and shot their beams straight as along the barrel of a rifle. The live interest of his look, and the slight but expressive play of his features, made up quite well for the occasional scarcity of words.

"Yes, everything is all ready," she said.

"Well, I won't keep you waiting long."

When he had rid himself of the lambs he strode down the slope to the spring, and presently she heard him "washing up" with more than his usual vigor. Pretty soon he came up and bore a beaming countenance to supper.

Janet, as she poured the coffee and passed the hot bread, gave an account of her day's work, telling first about the orphan and how she managed with him; then she took up the other lambs, consecutively.

"I got four altogether," she ended.

"Oh, you should not have done that."

"No?"

There was mingled surprise and disappointment in her look; but mainly disappointment.

"You could never have handled them that way—if they had been really coming fast. It would take a wagon. There is no use of your working like that."

"But," she insisted, after a pause, "you couldn't have carried more than those four, could you?"

"No—that was just about a load."

"And we got them all in, didn't we?"

"Oh, yes—yes. What I meant was that you oughtn't to work like that. But we certainly did get them all in. And it's the only way we could have done it. As it turned out, it was just the right thing to do—all that was necessary." After a moment's silence he felt he had not said quite enough. "You did first-class," he added. "The fact is, nobody could have done better."

Janet recovered her cheerfulness at once. She resumed her story of the day, and then, as she got around to the subject of the lamb again, she went into the shack and brought him out. Having been assured that he was looking well and was likely to recover, she sat down at her place again with the lamb in her lap. He lay there contentedly while she finished her supper.

"Yes," said Steve in answer to another of her questions, "lambs are kind of cute. Sometimes I feel bad for a lamb myself when his mother won't have anything to do with him. You ought to be out here later on, Miss Janet, when the

Charles D. Stewart

lambs have all been born and are starting to get frisky. That's when the fun begins."

"I have heard that lambs play together like children," she said.

"Oh, they do. You see they've got to learn jumping, too. And climbing—like a goat. That first lamb will soon be so lively that plain running won't be good enough for him. He'll want to do fancy tricks."

"Nature teaches them to play," observed Janet. "That's to give them practice and make them strong."

"I should say she did," said Steve, referring thus familiarly to Nature. "She puts all sorts of notions into their heads."

"What do they do, for instance, Mr. Brown?"

"Well, for one thing, a lamb likes to practice jumping. You see, sheep don't belong on prairies, like cattle. Cattle belong on prairies the same as buffalo, but sheep don't; they belong on mountains; that's the reason the young ones are so handy with their hoofs. They like to climb and jump, but on a prairie there isn't any place to jump off of. Well, maybe some day a lamb will be galloping and cavorting around, and he'll come across a hunk of rock salt that has been all licked off smooth on top and hollowed out. He'll take a running jump at that and land on it with all four hoofs in one spot and then he'll take a leap off the top. Then, when he sees what a good circus actor he is, he will gallop right around and do it over again; and the rest of his gang will start in and follow him, because what one sheep does the rest have got to do. That way they get to running in a circle round and round and taking turns at jumping."

"How perfectly funny!" exclaimed Janet.

"That's the way they do. They run races and play 'stump-the-leader' and 'hi-spy' and 'ring-around-the-rosy.' Why, Miss Janet, if you were out here a little later on, you would think it was *recess* all the time."

"I wish I might be," said Janet.

"A lamb likes to be on the go," he continued. "Sheep really ain't lively enough for a lamb, so he has to go off and have his own fun. He'll gallop around with a troop of other lambs and won't stop except long enough to go home for dinner."

"I don't see," said Janet, "how a lamb can go away like that and ever find his mother again, in such a crowd. They all look alike."

"That's easy enough. Every sheep's voice is keyed up to a different pitch; they all sound different some way or another. And every lamb has a little voice of his own."

"Yes, I've noticed that. But I didn't know there was any object in it. Or that they knew each other's voices."

"Oh, certainly they do. When a lamb gets hungry he whisks right around and runs into the flock and starts up his tune. She'll hear it and she'll start up too; and that way they'll keep signaling to each other. A lamb will run into a crowd of a thousand sheep and go right to his mother. When he has arrived, maybe she will smell him to make sure; and if he is all right, why—then it is all right."

"Then they don't ever go by looks, even when they're acquainted."

"Oh, no. They are different from people. They are not like you that know all the children by sight and don't have to call the roll. When a lamb wants to find a sheep, he just calls and she answers 'Present.'"

Steve Brown did not seem to lose sight of the fact that he was addressing his remarks to a school-teacher. While something of humor passed over his countenance at times, his attitude toward her was mainly sober and earnest. Janet, all absorbed in the subject of lambs, was in quite as serious a mood. She waited for him to continue; but he was not one to keep on indefinitely without questioning, not presuming, evidently, to know how much further she might be interested.

"She answers 'Present,'" repeated Janet. "Well, then; while they are answering each other, does she go to the lamb or does the lamb go to her?"

"Most likely they'll go to each other, and meet halfway. You see, that's the quickest way, When a lamb is hungry he wants his dinner right off."

"Then they are not any trouble in that way at all, are they!"

"Well—it's all easy enough after they have learned each other's voices. But at first they don't know that, and it takes them a little time to get it into their minds. That's when a herder has got trouble to keep things from getting mixed up. And if she has twins she has got to learn them both by heart."

"That's so—she would, wouldn't she!"

"Oh, yes. And twins learn to know each other, too. That's so they can go home to dinner together. For of course if she let one of them come alone it wouldn't be fair."

"Then sheep know that much!"

"I don't know that they do. I guess it's nature that tends to that, too. But there's a lot that nature is too busy to tend to. Then it's all up to the herder."

"Lambs are really quite dependent upon human care, then, aren't they?"

"Oh, yes. That is, if you want to try and save them all—like that one." He pointed to the occupant of her lap. "A lamb has got to get a meal right away, and a little sleep, and not get too chilled, or wet. Then if his mother and him stick together till they know each other by voice and smell, his chances are all right. After that you couldn't lose him."

"How long will it be, Mr. Brown, before everything is running that way?"

"It will start in just a few days. Just as soon as we get the lamb band going."

"The lamb band?" she queried.

"We have some lambs there in the corral now. Well, all that come to-morrow will go in with them, and in a day or two all that are strong and active will go out with their mothers and be the lamb band. All the others that haven't dropped lambs yet are called the drop band; they travel too much for lambs. Sheep with lambs ought to go out together and be handled separate. Well, whenever a lamb is born in the drop band, he is brought home to the corral; then when he knows things and is a little stronger he goes out with the lamb band; that way we keep advancing them right along, same as in school. First in the First Reader, then in the Second Reader, and so on."

"Oh, I see," said Janet, growing more deeply interested.

"And it isn't very long, of course, till they have all gone through and are in one band again. The lambs are all having a high old time and managing for themselves; and then one man can handle them again. The worst of the trouble is over, and there are not so many things to do all at once."

This seemed to exhaust the subject.

"What are you going to do to-morrow?" she inquired.

"Well, if I was sure that the herder was coming, I would just take them out and let the lambs drop behind, the same as to-day. Then if he brings the wagon along, as I told him to, he could get them in—that is, if there are a great many of them. There might not be many lambs come; but the trouble is that you can't tell. If I thought there were going to be a great many lambs, and he wasn't coming right away, I would keep the whole bunch here and not take them out at all—that is, I would if I had feed. But I could hardly feed twelve hundred sheep on a mere chance if I had it to spare. But then, I don't think he will stay away any longer. I'll just take them out."

"Really, it is quite a problem, isn't it?"

"That's just what I was beginning to think," he replied.

"How many lambs might there be in the next day or two, if they really started coming?"

"Maybe two or three hundred."

"Two or—!"

The words died out as Janet looked down in her lap and

considered the one. He was resting comfortably.

"Two—or—three—hundred," she repeated vacantly.

CHAPTER IX

G'lang there, yeoo-oo-oo, *Rip*. Yeoo-oo-oo, *Squat*. Yeoo-oo-oo—Buff.

Bang.

As it is difficult to make a noise in print, it might be well to explain that, of the above words, the last is supposed to sound like a revolver-shot. It is as near as we can come to the disturbance made by a Texas "prairie buster" as he came down Claxton road.

Ahead of him were ten oxen—five yoke. His far-reaching bull-whip exploded just beside Rip's left ear. The next shot took Squat exactly as aimed. There was a momentary scuffling of hoofs, an awful threat in the ox-driving language; then everything went on peacefully as before. The ox-driver caught the returning cracker deftly in two fingers of his right hand and settled down on his iron seat with his elbow on his knee while he took a chew of tobacco. The big tongue of his "busting" plow knocked in the ring of the wheelers' yoke; the chain clanked idly against it; a little cloud of debris—hair and dust which the cracker had bit out of the tuft between Squat's horns—floated away on the breeze.

All this was not done with any expectation of making them

go faster. For an ox to alter his gait, except slightly to run away, would be unnatural. It was merely to convey to certain ones that they were not out to enjoy the roadside grass. And to remind the string in general that the seat of authority was still being occupied.

For several days his voracious plowshare had been turning over the prairie in long ribbons of swath like the pages of a book. Texas in those days was turning over a new leaf; and such outfits as this did the turning. His last job had been to put an addition on a farm for an Ohio man about six miles out of town; he had turned forty more acres of tough prairie sod black side upwards and left behind him a dry dusky square in the horizon-girt green of the range. Being now homeward bound, he bent his sharp gray eyes upon the road ahead. The Claxton Road community, a moneyed streak in the population, was only half a mile away.

In the distance appeared a black man riding a broncho mule. It was Colonel Chase's man, Uncle Israel; he was coming along at an unsatisfactory pace, using his quirt regularly and remonstrating with the mule. As he drew near the head of the ox procession, the driver roared out a *Wo-o-o-o* in a tone which was intended to be understood as a general command; the powerful wheelers held back obediently and drew the chain tight in their efforts to stop; the rest of the string, after pulling them a short distance, also obeyed.

"Hello, Uncle."

"Good-mawnin', Mistah Hicks."

"How's things doing down home? Anything new?"

"Well—no, sah. Ev'ything jes' 'bout de same."

"Is the Colonel home?"

"No, sah. He's done gone to San Antone."

"Has he shipped yet?"

"Yes, sah."

"Who went up to Chicago with them?"

"Mistah Sattlee an' John Dick an' some mo'."

"Is Steve Brown at home?"

"No, sah. He's gone somewha's. An' he ain' come back. Mos' all de men folks is gone away."

"Has Miss Alice got back yet?"

"No, sah. She's off to de school-house in Boston yet. An' it ain't leff out. She's gwine be back dis spring."

"What's cattle bringing now?"

"Dunno, sah. I heah dey's done riz."

"Has little Johnnie Martin got his curls cut yet?"

"No, sah. Ah seed 'em on him."

"What's doing in town? Anything new there?"

"No, sah. Jes' 'bout de same as usual."

Uncle Israel, feeling that his information had not been very abundant, scratched his head and stirred his mind up thoroughly for news. He met the demand with two pieces of information.

"De railroad's done built a new loadin'-pen. An' dat high-tone bull took sick wif acclimatin'. But we's got him restin' easy now."

"The railroad's getting real extravagant, ain't it?" commented Jonas, turning his attention to the oxen again.

Having said a few words appropriate to the occasion of starting up, he flung out his bullwhip in a flourish of aerial penmanship and drove home the aforesaid remarks with a startling report. Again the bovine procession got under way.

In the course of time he came to where Claxton road ends and Claxton Road begins. It will be recalled that Claxton road, hemmed in by barb wire, leads interminably past vacant stretches of prairie with occasionally a farm and farmhouse. Nearing town its scene and atmosphere suddenly change. On the left are the ranchmen's home estates, with the stables and windmills and short avenues of china-berry trees leading up to comfortable porches; to the right, or facing these, is a large square of green with no roadside houses and no longer any confining fence. To any one who had come a long distance between the barb wires, this emergence upon the free, open common was very much as if he had been following a stream which, after long confinement to its course, opens out suddenly into a lake. This piece of land was not different from the prairie it had always been, except that the houses which faced it on all sides, as if it were a lake of the summer-resort variety, gave it an importance which was not its own. It was no more nor less than a square of primeval prairie whose owner, being satisfied with it, let it be as it was. Surrounded on all sides by real estate and other improvements, it held its own as immovably as if Texas had

Charles D. Stewart

here taken her last stand, in hollow square, against the encroachments of civilization. It belonged to Jonas Hicks. In the exact middle of it was the paintless frame house which we have already mentioned.

This structure is easily described. It consisted of a house with one room downstairs and one room upstairs. Its boarding was of the kind that runs up and down with battening strips at the cracks. Any one familiar with prairie architecture would see at once that the owner, having a house to build, had gone straightway to work and erected a herder's shack on a residential scale and put some windows in it. Because of its porchlessness it seemed rather tall, as if it had grown after it was built or had stretched itself up to get a better view; and the single window in the end of the upper story gave it a watchful appearance. This watchful window, which might be said to mark its front, looked toward the residences along Williston Road.

The cottages which faced this place on the side toward town were confined to "lots" along an unpaved street. Across on Claxton Road town lots grew to the size of country estates and looked more commanding. But the shack house, with its twenty acres of elbow room, rather commanded them all, especially as its central position marked the common as its own grounds. Being tall and upright and spare, like a Texan, it had an attitude toward them like that of a pioneer drill-master; it seemed to be standing out on the drill-grounds with the other houses all marshaled up before it and toeing the social line.

The place was given shape and form entirely by the other property, all of which was fenced on its own side of the highway, the owner of the twenty acres never having shut it off from the roads which passed along two sides of it. This hospitable openness was a fortunate thing for the traveling public, affording as it did a short cut to town. Quite a little of the traffic that came down Williston Road turned out and followed the trail which led diagonally across it past the door of the house. And usually the traveler, whether horseman or driver, would speak in passing; or, more likely, stop to have a talk with Jonas Hicks, who, if he were at home, might be engaged in plaiting a whip or mixing batter for pancakes or taking a stitch in his clothes, the iron seat of a "prairie-busting" plow being particularly hard on the seat of a man's trousers. It was to this place that the plowman was bending his homeward way.

Eventually, as oxen always do, they arrived. Having navigated them up to the kitchen door and brought them to a stop with a stentorian *Wo*, he unhooked the wheelers, dropped the chain from each yoke, and turned them loose to graze or lie down as each pair might decide; then he went around the corner of the house and set to work making a fire in the stove. It was an outdoor stove of the locomotive variety, having two large iron wheels upon which it had traveled thousands of miles in the service of the J. W. Cattle Company. Mr. Hicks had fastened its tongue or handle to a staple in the chimney of the house, for which chimney it had no use, having a smoke-stack of its own.

When the stove was belching forth smoke he turned his attention to the inside of the house. Presently he came out with a pan of flour and various kitchen utensils which he placed on a bench beside the door; then he drew a bucket of water and proceeded to mix pancake batter. He had not accomplished much when he was interrupted. Just when the batter was mixed to the right consistency, and the first spoonful was ready to go on, a little girl appeared. She had a pie which she bore before her with a look of great responsibility.

Charles D. Stewart

"Ma says maybe you would like to have a pie."

"Why, how do, Susie. How's Susie getting along these days?"

"Real well," replied Susan, holding the pie up higher.

Mr. Hicks bent his tall Texas form in the middle and took it from her. The pie had the outlines of a star in its centre by way of a vent-hole; the edges were nicely crimped.

"It's a mighty good-looking pie. What does that stand for, Susie?" he asked, holding the pie up so that she could view its face and placing his finger upon its centre.

"That stands for Texas," answered Susan promptly.

Mr. Hicks put the pie on the bench and sat down beside it with his elbows on his knees.

Something like a smile betrayed itself in the lean muscles of his jaw and showed somehow around his large aggressive chin.

"How does it come that you didn't go to school to-day, Susie?" He pointed to the white frame school-house which occupied a corner of his place.

"'Cause," answered Susan, by way of complete explanation.

"That's a mighty good reason. If I had an excuse like that I wouldn't go to school myself. How's your ma? Is she well?"

"Yes, sir. Only she had a kinda headache this morning, and I wiped the dishes."

"You did? How did you know so quick that I was back?

Were you watching for me so that you could bring over the pie?"

"Oh!" exclaimed Susan, "we heard you coming. We could hear you saying bad words when you was 'way up the road."

A change suddenly came over the spirit of Mr. Hicks's physiognomy. He sat stroking his wide-spreading moustache. Jonas Hicks had a self-made moustache which seemed to have borrowed its style from the horns of a Texas steer. It might be said that, for the moment, he looked serious; but you could never tell from his face exactly what his emotions were. It was against his principles to be caught laughing, and yet his solemnity was somewhat radiant despite him.

Suddenly he rose and went into the house. In a little while he reappeared carrying a milk-pan filled with comb-honey. It was white honey which the bees had deposited in his useless chimney; the sirup filled the pan almost to its edge, while the middle was piled high with oozing chunks of comb. He placed it on the bench beside him. The eyes of Susan opened wide as she saw this sight. He talked about one thing and another and asked her many inconsequential questions. After much tantalizing talk on Mr. Hicks's part, she learned that the honey was for her and that she was to take it all home with her.

Susan was for starting home at once.

"What' s your hurry, Susie? Won't you stay a while and have a piece of pie?"

"I'd rather I'd have a pancake," said Susan, looking furtively at the smoking griddle.

He rose at once and put on a large spoonful of batter. When the cake was ready to turn, he caused it to turn a somersault with a quick toss of the griddle; then he spread it evenly with honey and rolled it into the form of a cylinder with the honey inside.

"There, now, Susie. That's what I call a joof-lickum *tamale*. It's pancake *de la verandah*. Watch out that you don't burn your fingers."

He set the griddle temporarily aside and sat down again. While Susan ate, she leaned across his tall knee and looked up at him admiringly.

"I like your pancakes," she volunteered. "Your pancakes has got fringe on them."

Mr. Hicks's countenance took on more of an expression around the eyes; he regarded her with deep interest.

"All the boys at school like your pancakes, too," she continued. "They are coming over some other recess when you are home, and you can make them all a pancake again. Will you put honey on their pancakes?"

"For boys!" exclaimed Susan's heroine in great surprise. "No honey for boys. Honey is only for girls."

"And mas too," added Susan. "Ain't honey for mas too?"

"Doesn't your ma make them with fringe on?" inquired Jonas, in hope of making a new start.

Susan vouchsafed no reply. The subject stood in abeyance while she feasted and took thought. Presently her attention rested upon the griddle. On it there was a diminutive pancake which had made itself from the drippings of an overgenerous spoonful.

"I like little pancakes too," she hinted.

Jonas took it off and presented it to her.

"There, Susie. When you go home you can give that to your dollie."

Susan's eyes seemed to expand as she turned them up to Mr. Hicks, the source of supernal illumination. If the pancake had seemed desirable, this wonderful *idea* was ten times as much of a present. Her bliss grew visibly deeper as she looked first at the pancake and then at the resourceful Mr. Hicks. She was so completely won that she consented to sit on his knee. There she resumed her *tamale* in the intervals of conversation.

"Mr. Hicks. How did the bees come to go down your chimbly?"

"'Cause," replied Mr. Hicks.

"Oh, *Mister* Hicks—tell me *why* the bees went down your chimbly. I want to know why."

"I guess they thought it was an old hollow tree."

"Do you think maybe they would think our chimbly was an old hollow tree? Oh, I wish they would come down our chimbly."

"Oh, they wouldn't come down your chimney. That wouldn't do at all."

Charles D. Stewart

"Why wouldn't they, Mr. Hicks?"

"'Cause," answered Jonas, still pretending to be taciturn and mysterious.

"Oh, Mister *Hicks*. *Please* don't talk that way. Tell me why."

"Because," explained Mr. Hicks, "bees would know better than that. If they came and stopped your chimney all up with honey, how would Santa Claus ever get down? Who gave you the dolly?"

"Santa Claus."

"Well, don't you see if the chimney was all full of honey he would get it all over his clothes? And all over *her* clothes? And besides, he would get his whiskers all chock-full of honey. How would you like to have your curls all full of molasses?"

As he made this remark he lifted a curl and contemplated it, the truth being that he was not nearly so much interested in the honey as in her hair. He made these remarks simply by way of sticking to the subject. Susan, conscious of her curls, gave her head a toss which sent them flying about her face, one side and then the other; then she took another bite and returned to her speculations.

"Did the bees know that you haven't got any little girl?"

Mr. Hicks was inclined to sanction the idea that the bees had this view of the uselessness of his chimney. The subject of his girllessness leading on to another case of "why," he fell back promptly upon the hollow tree theory pure and simple; the which he took pains to establish by stories of trees filled with honey and of terrible big bears that lived in the trees and ate the honey. He was going on to consider the advantages of living in a hollow tree—with a good strong door to it—when a new game offered itself.

Leaning forward and turning his head to see how the stove was doing, the end of his long moustache stroked Susan under the chin and drew a fine trail of titillation across her throat. To the surprise of the owner of the "whiskers," she clapped her chin to her shoulder and shrank from the excruciating touch. Before long Mr. Hicks had occasion to turn his head to the other side. This time it tickled even more and Susan had to giggle. After that a surprising number of things, of all imaginable sorts, demanded his attention on one side or the other, and every time the moustache acted in the same manner, much to the surprise of the innocent Mr. Hicks. As soon as that beard developed its full powers of tickling, it took effect wherever it touched, and Susan had to protect herself by grabbing the moustache and pushing Mr. Hicks's face, which face seemed able to stand any amount of rough usage. When finally his every move produced such paroxysms of laughter that she could stand it no longer, Susan squirmed out of his arms. Then, with sudden seriousness, she picked up the doll's pancake which had fallen from her hand. Their visit thus brought to an end, Jonas did not try to renew it; he was growing hungry. He gave her the pan of honey and placed her hands so that she would hold it level.

"There, now, Susan. Be careful that you don't fall down and get any of it in your mouth."

Susan, who was nobody's fool, knew that Mr. Hicks sometimes made remarks which were purposely foolish. This one engaged her mind for a moment as if she hoped to make head and tail of it, but as it seemed to be unanswerable she gave him an amused look and started for home.

As Susan neared her front gate another visitor was approaching—this time from the direction of Claxton Road. It was Mrs. Norton; she had in mind to get the rockery returned. Jonas, watching Susan to see whether she got home with the honey unspilt, was oblivious to the half of the world that was behind his back; but when he turned about and took up the dish of batter, intending to pour out a griddleful of pancakes, he saw her coming. Immediately he seized the pie and hurried it into the house. By the time he came out she had arrived.

"Good-morning, Mrs. Norton."

"Good-morning, Mr. Hicks. Have you got all through with your work?"

"All except sewing on a few buttons. Ploughing is all done for the present, I guess."

"Mr. Hicks, we have been wondering whether you could do us a little favor. The ladies of the Chautauqua Circle have been studying geology,—the earth, you know,—and we needed some stones for specimens—samples. And of course stones are not very plentiful around here—"

"Why don't you go and take some out of Steve Brown's rockery? Help yourself, as God says."

"Why, that's just what we did do. We were passing there, and we each took one—without particularly thinking. They are lying behind Colonel Chase's big gate. We got them up there, but found they were rather heavy. Could we get you to haul them back for us?"

"I bet you could, Mrs. Norton. The next time I pass there with the wagon I'll put them on. I don't suppose those stones are in any particular hurry, are they?"

"Well," said Mrs. Norton, taking thought, "I have been thinking that perhaps it would be just as well to get them back before he comes home. He is out at the Thompson ranch tending to those sheep again, you know."

"Did you hear whether any one went with him?"

"Well, no—er—yes. That is, I don't really know whether there is or not. I heard there was somebody out there."

Her answer, or the manner of it, struck Jonas as peculiar.

"Extra herder or two?" he suggested.

"One of the boys who was out at the ranch told somebody in town that there was somebody out there. The regular herder was up at the county-seat and hadn't got back."

Mrs. Norton, now that she had boggled, by surprise, into the acknowledgment that she knew anything whatever about the matter, felt herself in a problematical position. She did not know whether his question had been accidental or not; it sounded as if he knew; possibly he had put it as a feeler to discover whether she knew. In which case the subject became rather difficult; she did not know whether to dissemble, nor how much to dissemble, nor how to do it.

Jonas, his curiosity aroused, persevered with more inquiries. Mrs. Norton, after answering with a few vague references to Tuck Reedy's report, suddenly made a bald evasion of the subject; she went back without ceremony to the subject of rocks. Jonas had a new feeling that there was something peculiar about the matter.

"And so I was thinking," continued Mrs. Norton, "that we had better return them pretty soon. It was really an improper thing for us to do—though we did not particularly think of it at the time. If he came home and found the rockery gone he might not like it."

"Steve is rather peculiar, some ways," remarked Jonas.

"Is he? In what way?"

This remark of his had seemed to bear upon the hidden subject. She had hope of receiving moral enlightenment from the masculine standpoint.

"Mostly about rocks. Did you ever hear about the time I hauled that tombstone for him?"

"I knew you did, of course. What did he do?"

"Well, he didn't do anything much. He expected me to drive oxen without using any strong language. Just took a sudden notion he didn't want it. I had got that stone loaded onto a strong truck that I had rigged up apurpose; then I started up and got the cattle headed up Main Street in fine shape. Steve was coming along on the sidewalk. All of a sudden he stepped out into the road and spoke to me. He said he didn't like the sound of it and he wished I'd leave out the swearing. He said it rather cool and solemn, like Pastor Gates does when he says to omit the second stanza. For a minute I didn't know what to think. I was doing a plain job of ox-driving and I told him so. 'That's all right; I understand that,' he says. 'But you don't expect to go cussing into that cemetery, do you?' 'Well—no,' I says. 'Not since you mention it.' For a minute he had me where I couldn't go ahead nor back up. A man has got to use language to oxen, and what is he going to say? I am so used to it that I don't even hear myself, unless I stop to listen; and so it doesn't mean any more than the oxen understand by it. And that isn't much. 'No,' I says, 'not since you mention it.' 'Well, then,' he says, 'you might as well quit now. Afterwards you can drive them any way you please and say anything you want. But it doesn't sound right to me now, and I don't want any swearing on this job.' He said it in such a way that I could see just about how he felt about it. I saw that any more of it wouldn't do. I guess I ought to 'a' thought of it myself."

"And did you succeed in doing as he wished?" asked Mrs. Norton.

"Well, I managed to get them there somehow—considering I hadn't had any time to practice. It made me wonder, though, what a deaf and dumb man would think if he got a job driving oxen."

"And that is what you mean by his being peculiar?"

"That's sort of it. But maybe that one doesn't quite cover the point. What I mean is that he's got all sorts of notions of what's right and wrong; and he tells it to you all of a sudden. He's quicker 'n pig-tail lightning."

"Do you suppose he might think it wrong for us to meddle with his property?"

"Oh, no. He isn't that way. You know how he is about such things. And besides he wouldn't be likely to say anything. I only mentioned that tombstone business because his mother set so much store by the rockery. He looks at that as a sort of a monument."

A look of deep seriousness came over Mrs. Norton's countenance. It deepened as she thought.

"Of course, Mr. Hicks, we intended to tell him about it—and thank him for the use of the stones. But possibly it would be more considerate not to say anything about it."

"Not tell him at all," repeated Jonas reflectively.

"But I suppose that no matter how we put them back he would notice that it had been changed."

"Yes. I guess he knows it by heart. He had those blue-flower vines started on it."

"It was really very thoughtless of us," mused Mrs. Norton.

"Oh, well; it isn't anything serious," remarked Jonas. "If he seems serious about it you can blame me. Tell him I told you to. I'm really part owner anyway; I discovered a lot of those stones and put them there. He'll understand how it was. And if he says anything to me I'll tell him I didn't think. If you want me to I'll make it all right when I go out there this afternoon."

"Are you going out there?" she asked, looking up with sudden interest.

"I've been thinking I would. I want to drop out those three middle yoke and let them run on grass a while. While I'm out there, I guess I'll make Steve a call and stop overnight. It'll be late when I get there."

"Oh!"

She saw a very lively and interesting picture of Mr. Hicks's arrival at the shack. He would not be a very welcome visitor, she thought. Having the misconceptions she did of affairs at the ranch, she saw all sorts of possibilities; she said nothing, however, which would keep this interesting three-cornered meeting from taking place. She turned the conversation at once into other channels. Having answered his inquiries regarding neighborhood affairs, and having been finally assured that he would return the rockery and make everything "all right," she took her leave.

Jonas had had no very definite intention of undertaking the journey at once; but now that his mind was turned in that direction, he saw that to-day was as good as to-morrow, or even the day after; he fired up the stove and again took the batter in hand. This time the pancakes went ahead without interruption. When he had stacked up the requisite number, and eaten them with honey and bacon, he hooked the wheelers to the wagon, and then added the rest of the cattle, yoke after yoke. The plough was to remain where it was. Ensconced upon the more altitudinous seat of authority he swung his lash out with a report like a starting-gun and made his way, with the necessary language, across the open and up Claxton Road.

Jonas's trip to the ranch took longer than it takes to tell it. But there is not, in truth, anything about the trip itself to tell—and yet there ought to be some way of describing time. Under the circumstances, and especially as oxen cannot be hurried, it might be well to pass the time by talking about Jonas Hicks's past; it will be better than to take up the scenery again. In those parts the scenery, if the weather remains settled, is rather uneventful; it is the same when you arrive as when you started. On a prairie the human mind carries its own scenery.

Jonas Hicks's past had been somewhat variegated and thus all of a piece. Some years before the present moment, when the railroad was younger and the "garden spot of the world" was just beginning to attract attention to its future, Jonas carelessly acquired a patch of forty acres near the new town of Thornton. At that time he was still "on the drive," a vocation which took him with the big herds anywhere from Texas to Fort Benton in Montana. In the calling of cowboy he had, by a process of natural selection, risen and gradually settled into the character of cook. Risen, we say, because, in a cattle outfit, there is not a more important and unquestioned personage; his word is law and they call him pet names. However, from the day he got down out of the saddle, in an emergency, and consented to act in the capacity of "Ma,"—which was a joke,—he was in continual demand as cook, with increasing popularity. Though he still claimed the ability to ride and rope and hog-tie with the best of them, he was thenceforth a cook with all the cook's perquisites and autocratic say-so. There is nowhere, we might observe, so deep an indication of the true power of Woman as this respect that is paid to her position, even when it is being occupied by a red-faced being who wears whiskers and who has no real right, of his own, to be anything more than an equal of his brother man. But the cook's laws must not be disobeyed; they allow him to make laws because he is cook; masculine sentiment is on his side; human welfare demands it. As Jonas was popular in the position, and did not mind the work when it was appreciated, he continued to fry bacon and fringy flapjacks and, in general, to furnish "the grease of life," as he called it, to the outfit. And while he was doing it his fellows conducted the beef, on ten thousand legs, from the South to the North. They took them North so that they would put on fat under the stimulus of a Northern winter.

In those days he engineered the peculiar cookstove which we have already noticed. It was a big, square, sheet-iron stove with an iron axle and wheels like those of a sulky plow. This piece of machinery was hooked on behind the chuckwagon, which it followed from clime to clime. Jonas, being a live man and a "hustler," seldom waited for the outfit to reach the camping-place and come to a halt before starting to get a meal. As he explained, he had to get about a two-mile start on their appetites, with pancakes; and so, while the stove was yet far off from its destination, he would fire up and get things going. Then he would trot along behind and cook. While "she" (the stove) lurched into buffalo wallows and rode the swells and unrolled the smoke other stack far out across the billowy prairie, Jonas would hurry along behind and keep house. Entirely occupied with his kitchen duties he would move busily here and there or remain steadily behind or beside the stove while it pursued its onward way, and with the bucket of batter in his hand and the griddle smoking and sizzling, he would seldom miss a flap. From the standpoint of a weary cowboy it was a beautiful sight. It is, indeed, a pleasant thing, when you are tired and hungry, to see your supper thus coming along as conqueror over space and time.

No one but a man like Jonas, who had the combined talents of a sea-cook and a cowboy, could have managed it. To make coffee under such circumstances took considerable ability, of course. And even the flapjacks, which stayed on the stove better, might seem difficult. Jonas, however, was a man of quick hand and eye; things seldom got the drop on him, and he handled the pancakes with a revolver wrist. As the foreman said, he was "a first-class culinary engineer." In doing this, his longtime experience on bucking bronchos stood him in good stead; then, too, his practice was confined almost entirely to pancakes and coffee, for they were but few and simple dishes that he knew by heart. But even with this special expertness it took a quick man and a philosopher, especially when the stove cut a caper and the footing was uneven. As Jonas once remarked when he stepped amiss on his high boot-heel and spilled all the batter into a buffalo wallow, "This is certainly a corrugated country." He was not always and necessarily a profane man, whatever one might think who heard him driving oxen. In times of real trouble he expressed himself coolly and then stuck to the facts.

For a long time Jonas thought little of the small patch of prairie which belonged to him; he only began to take it seriously when he sold twenty acres—a deal which was consummated through the agency of Stephen Brown, senior, who paid the taxes in his absence and thus knew, generally, where Jonas was. Coming back a year or two later he was surprised to see how that place had built up; and when, after repeated visits, he had made himself known to all the neighbors and discovered what nice people they were,—it was a new sensation for Jonas to have neighbors,—he got it more and more into his head that they were *his* neighbors, and that he belonged there. He decided to settle down in those parts. Things in general seemed to be shifting into a new mode of life and impelling him to go along. In the early eighties, central Texas was becoming tightly fenced; the barb wire was spreading out generally; railroads were hauling herds where formerly they went afoot; shorthorn bulls were changing the face of nature; it was plain to be seen that before a great while the long drives would be a thing of the past. While there was still use for the cowboy, there was less call for Jonas's peculiar abilities.

Having land which seemed to call for a house, he built one on it; but at first he did not occupy it himself. During his absences it was occupied by "white" families of the sort that move often by wagon and work cotton on shares; meantime his fancy was playing about the place and taking root. Coming back in the fall the house was vacant. As Jonas was himself an excellent wife and a kind husband, he moved in. Having in mind to stop a while, he of course stopped at his own house.

The problem of living on one spot solved itself in the most natural manner. Instead of driving cattle in the old way, he conquered a few and drove them from the seat of a plow. Thus while everything was going forward, he mounted the wheel of Progress and put his hand to the throttle; and now every time he got back from one of his occasional absences a new farm had been opened up forever and ever. But it must not be thought that he had himself become an agriculturist. He had not even dreamed of it. There is not necessarily any more relation between a "prairie buster" and the land he "busts" than there is between a farmer and a locomotive engineer; the spirit of it is different. Jonas bossed cattle.

If there would seem to be anything of incongruity or humorous contrast between Jonas and his married neighbors, it must be remembered that, under the circumstances of a growing country, there was not. In a land where many men live alone in shacks and do their own work, and where any woman's husband must be able to go forth with a frying-pan and shift for himself at times, it was no marvel to see Jonas Hicks doing the same; though, to be sure, he was doing it a little nearer town than is customary, and this proximity made his single-blessedness shine out a little plainer. But if there was any humor in that, or in fact anything else, it was Jonas's prerogative to see it first and to stretch the joke as far as it would go. Then, too, he lived there only at intervals—which were getting to cover the greater part of the time—in the style of a man who camps out. And after a few days' absence in "busting," he would suddenly reappear and turn loose his oxen and start up housekeeping with all the new pleasure of a man who is glad to get back among the folks again.

From all of which it will be seen that Jonas's house needed to make no apology for its presence; he had owned land there among the first; it was the others who were the innovators and the newcomers; and as to his way of housekeeping it simply clung a little closer to nature. It was, in fact, the most natural thing in the neighborhood.

Charles D. Stewart

As he continued to live there he liked it more and more. He was glad that things turned out just as they did. His very location in "the middle of the puddle," as Steve Brown put it, made it look, to him, as if all these beautiful women and interesting little children had gathered round to ornament his position in life; and there is a great deal in looks. He felt also, having owned some of the land upon which the towns-people were settled, that he was in some manner responsible for it all; and so he had a corresponding pride in the community at large and was personally interested in everybody's welfare.

His own property he could have sold or cultivated; but he was well enough satisfied with things as they were. He could have put up a sign, "keep off the grass"; he could have built a fence or forbidden any one to use his place as a short cut to town; he could have done anything that goes with private ownership; but with him ownership was not necessarily private. To a man with such large Texas views and lifelong experience of "free grass," such carefulness of a mere twenty acres would seem rather small, especially small as directed against such neighbors. He was pleased to be numbered among them, and he acted accordingly. If the minister's wife needed temporary pasturage for her real shorthorn cow, just arrived from the North, he invited her to use his place permanently; he rather liked to see cows around. If an incoming herd of cattle wished to halt there they were welcome; it reminded him of old times. If the whole surrounding country went "cross-lots" over his land, there was no objection; what difference did it make? And besides, it was the farmers and ranchmen who gave him employment.

He would not sell any land, though. Right here was where he exercised his private right. He liked things well enough as they were. But when the proposition came up to purchase a small site for a school-house, he presented them with a small piece off the corner, only asking that they refrain from putting a fence around it. As this restriction was no drawback to the community, they readily acceded to it; consequently the children played ball or did whatever they pleased all over the place, much to his entertainment. At recess the youngsters spent much of their time around him, if he were at home, and though this interfered considerably with his housework he did not mind the delay.

However difficult it might be to name his particular function in the social organism, he had certainly made a place for himself; and it was wonderful, as time went on, how large that place grew to be. Any woman, when her husband is away from home, is likely to face situations which make sudden call for a Man. In a neighborhood where husbands and hired men were frequently away at the ranch, this state of affairs was always breaking out somewhere, and Jonas, occupying his prominent position as next door neighbor to everybody, and being naturally adapted to act in that capacity, was always the Man. His very geographical situation was sufficient to turn the mind towards him, but the particular reason for that heliotropism on the part of his feminine neighbors was that he was an easy man for a woman to ask. Being asked, he always served her in a spirit of masculine banter and then went away as if he had enjoyed the joke. Thus she could be grateful for his neighborly turn without feeling herself under any painful state of obligation. Naturally his custom grew. One moment he would be mending a yoke or plaiting a lash, the next moment he would be clapping himself on a broncho to outdodge an escaped bull, or dashing up the road to put out a prairie fire before it reached the stable; he could lift a stove or drive a nail or spade up a little place for flower seed; he could do any one of these things in about a minute and then have time to sit down and have a good neighborly visit. Possibly his familiarity with cookstove affairs had brought him nearer to

Charles D. Stewart

woman's point of view. He looked like a Texas Ranger, and was just as generally useful, but in a more domestic way. And yet he had been good with a six-shooter. So times change; and men with them.

Altogether, he might be best described simply as Jonas Hicks; his position being one that he naturally fell into. And he filled the position of Jonas Hicks the same as if he were a policeman or a priest or a fire department. In time of trouble it was only necessary for a woman to ask. Indeed, his trade with woman grew to such proportions that he had been obliged, on more than one occasion, to cancel an engagement with a man in order that he might do something for his wife. And he stated the case in just about that way.

Chivalry is not entirely a thing of the past. It is a virtue which grows wild in Texas. When it is domesticated with the ox, and pursues the even tenor of everyday life, it is a most useful institution.

With all this talk of ours, it is doubtful if we have brought the oxen a mile on their way. At this point we shall go on ahead.

It will be easy enough to reach the next chapter before he does.

CHAPTER X

Repeatedly, Janet had misjudged her fellow man's motives and had to correct her theory of him. It was, however, his own fault. He had a way of going ahead without making explanations. He seemed deficient in that sort of guile which would prompt a man to forefend suspicion of his motives, or else he did not think it necessary, or, worse still, did not care; and so his "high-handedness," as it had at first appeared to her, took sinister color from her unusual situation and his too easy advantage. Now she had about arrived at the comfortable conclusion that Steve Brown was simply one who saw what ought to be done and did it.

His acts had a way of doing their own explaining, uninterpreted by him, so that, as they sorted together in that prairieful of time, he became a less difficult study; and by the time she had thus learned him she found herself in a most comfortable case. He was really a very simple sort of man to understand, after all. While he had been very alarming at first she had come to see into his mental state, and she liked, or at least had grown accustomed to, his faults.

His lack of talkativeness had made the process seem rather slow at first, and she had felt that more talk would have helped; but now she had begun to think differently. She had thought him wanting in tact, but the fact of the matter was

Charles D. Stewart

that he did not need it. He did better without it. She reflected, however, that his qualities were of the kind that would easily remain undiscovered by other women. One had to know him. He had been quite a revelation to her, perfectly simple. It was no longer he that seemed strange to her, but rather the adventure itself,—especially when she reflected that it happened such a little while ago. He seemed to date back farther than that; indeed, her knowing of him did not seem to be a thing of any date at all. And yet he owed his existence, so far as she was concerned, to that mere chance and her sudden dash out into the distance. It is strange how things happen.

What had been his history up to the time that had happened? This question had passed across her mind and brought with it a shade of doubt; but it soon lost itself in his real presence; he was simply Steve Brown.

She felt that she knew him. And now, on this evening, when he had entertained her with his explanation of the ways of sheep, there came a pause. After a while he rose to tend the fire, which had burnt low. He scraped the embers together and put on the wood, and then, having sat down again, he told her, rather deliberately, that on that day he had caught her horse.

He had not broached this subject during all this time. And at supper, before they became so interested in talking, there had been plenty of opportunity. He went on to explain that he had not caught the horse exactly; he had rather got it without the trouble of catching. The animal had been so willing to form his acquaintance that it had only been necessary to lay hold of him.

"And where is he now?" She was puzzled.

"I put him in an old sheep corral near the place I got him. I've been thinking I ought to go and get him to-night. That is, if you are not afraid to stay alone."

Why had he not informed her of this before? Would not any one naturally have done so? Here she was in this place all on account of the escape of her horse; and yet he had not told her about this. There was something strange here. Could it be that he would stoop to deceit!

Janet immediately—what she would not have believed she would do—brought him to an accounting.

"Mr. Brown," she said sternly, "why did you not tell me of this before?"

"Well, Miss Janet, the point-blank truth is that I thought I would rather spend the evening here."

He blenched perceptibly as he said it. Janet, seeing him now in a state of mild propitiation, became suddenly aware of the schoolmistress tone in which she had made him own up; and as he considered what way to answer, she was more at a loss than he was.

"And besides," he added, with more assurance, "I intended to go for him after you had gone to bed and say nothing about it. You might be afraid if you knew I was not around— though there isn't any danger of anything. But just now I got to thinking it over and when it came to the point, I did not like to go away without your knowing it. I thought I ought to tell you."

"Oh—that was it!"

"You see I didn't have any rope or bridle along when I

caught him; so I just put him in the corral. And I couldn't bring him home by the forelock when I had my arms full of lambs. I caught him just before noon. If he waited till I got around to him again in the regular course of herding, he would be pretty bad off for a drink."

This statement of the case decided her at once. As far as her own needs were concerned, she could not ride the horse without a saddle even if she dared mount him again, which she would not; but when she considered the animal's thirst she decided to set her night fears aside.

"No; of course you could not bring him home that way. If you wish to go for him I can stay here. I am not at all afraid."

"There isn't really anything to be afraid of," he said, rising. He paused a moment, regarding her seriously. "I *could* go for him in the morning before I take the sheep out. But you see I would have to start so early that it would still be night anyway."

"Oh, I shall not be afraid at all, Mr. Brown. There is nothing to be afraid of."

This was how it happened that Janet, a while later, was sitting alone gazing at the North Star. She was looking at that star in particular because Steve Brown had called her attention to it by way of proving that he would be able to find his way back to her. At intervals her eye let go of the star and came back to the fire.

"*I thought I ought to tell you.*"

Why ought? If there was no danger at all, and he felt that she would be afraid, why did he change his mind? This interested her. For a time the darkness was neglected.

Evidently he had planned this and had no doubts. If a woman is afraid to be alone in the dark, and there is no danger at all, the most considerate course is to go away when she is sleeping. He had his ideas of dealing with women. Why then had he found any difficulty in doing it with her? "I thought I *ought* to tell you."

She had said she would not be the least bit afraid. And so she was not—at first. Before long, however, the Night insisted upon being seen and heard. Space and darkness began to demand human attention. Unable to do otherwise, she looked up and contemplated the big blackboard of night, and especially the North Star, to which the front stars of the Dipper served as a pointer. And very soon she was wholly engaged upon the silence.

It is no small thing, if you are not used to it, to occupy a lone prairie at night. You face the absence of the whole human race. The ominous stillness centres upon you with all the weight of Past, Present, and Future. You are sitting up with the universe. And while you sit there, and keep watch, you feel like the last survivor. Night burns her solemn tapers over the living and the dead; there is now room for anything to happen.

Suddenly and without warning, an awful outburst of language sprang from the very throat of Night and claimed the starry silence for its own. It was a clap of language which, coming so unexpectedly, seemed to make the stars all blink at once. Then fell a hush much deeper than the silence of before. There was a moment of suspense; then a sharp gunlike report which seemed to crack the silence but not to break it. Again the threatening voice sounded—this time nearer and more violent.

Janet sprang to her feet and made for the shack—not

Charles D. Stewart

forgetting, fortunately, the lamb. Being inside, she dropped the lamb on the bunk and shut the door.

She had noticed in the corner that morning a narrow roof-board which might have been used to hold the door shut; she felt for it at once. When she had it in her hands, at last, she put one end against the door and braced the other end against the wall opposite where it met the floor. The board was so long that it would not go low enough to catch securely against the door. She managed, however, by pressing down hard on its middle, to spring it tightly into place. There being nothing further to be done, except to keep as still as possible and hope for the best, she proceeded to do so.

The lamb being less discreet, lifted its voice and called out for its mother. There was an answering cry from the corral, after which there seemed to be promise of quiet. Janet held her breath and got what reassurance she could out of the fact that she was surrounded by walls, between the shrunk boards of which the glare of the fire showed in vertical streaks. As it was pitch dark inside, she could see nothing of her protecting structure except in so far as it had the appearance of being a cage of fire.

The threatening voice advanced by stages, coming surely on. Presently she could hear the tramp of many feet, accompanied by the clanking of chains. There was a dull knocking of heavy wheels. There was the sharp crack of the whip-lash again, a quicker trampling of hoofs, a louder sound of wheels and chains and a still louder vociferation of commands. Janet could hardly have felt less confidence in that shack if it had been the heavy artillery that was coming into position— which it sounded very much like. There some sort of evolution performed and a command to stop; then all was silent again. For a space, Janet heard nothing.

Then a sound of footfalls told her that he was coming nearer. The door was tried. When it did not open he pushed it harder. It gave a little at the top, but, to her great relief, the brace held. After a little she heard his measured tramp again. And again there was silence.

Janet, unable to endure the suspense, put her eye to the knot-hole. The intruder, a tall piratical-looking figure, was standing between her and the fire; she could see his general build in black. From the side of his face there protruded a terrible moustache.

The man, after a period of silent thought, went and fetched some wood. He was going to take possession of the fire. Janet kept her eye to the knot-hole. When he had the fire burning better, he straightened up and wandered round to the other side of it. At this, the sinister silhouette, acting as a sort of dissolving view, came out in favor of the old maxim that "there is a bright side to everything." It was no less a person than Jonas Hicks. Little Jimmie Wanger's "Misser Donas!"

"Misser Donas dimme pop,"—Janet's mind took a jump to this. Morning and night she had heard the sentence reiterated by the diminutive Jimmie, the interpretation of which was, according to Rosie, that Mr. Hicks had at one time presented Jimmie with a ball of pop-corn. It was the only sentence Jimmie's mind cared to communicate. As it was the only thing in life worth mentioning, he brought it out upon every occasion; thus it had become recorded on her mind with phonographic unforgettableness, and when she saw Mr. Hicks through the knot-hole his act of benevolence repeated itself in the same words. The sight of this benefactor in the guise of a cursing desperado made a clash among the ideas in her mind; but Jimmie's sentence came out on top.

Besides hearing about him in this way, she had once had the

honor of meeting Mr. Hicks himself—this time also in connection with his leaning toward children. He stopped at her schoolyard pump for a drink, and having taken it he put his head in at the door and smiled—a thing he never did upon compulsion. Being invited to enter, he did so, taking the visitors' chair near the rostrum; and when she asked him, according to the time-honored custom, whether he would not like to address a few words to the school, he did that also, standing his whip up in the corner and giving some very engaging advice upon the subject of education, part of which, being of a hidden nature, was evidently intended for the entertainment of the teacher. In this way he had been her one and only visitor; and then, having had his jocose presence so repeatedly called to mind at the Wangers', she had become disabled to think of him as anything but the ministering angel of pop-corn.

Now her sole concern was to put in her appearance in as graceful a manner as possible. Whatever sort of man he might really be, she knew he was a person of quick intelligence who would certainly see any indications of her taking fright at him. She wished to emerge at once, smoothly and naturally. But when she put her hands to the tight roofing-board she discovered that there was going to be difficulty in the operation.

At first she tried to lift it by taking hold near the middle. As the board had been bent down by her pressing it into place, her lifting only made it grip tighter. It resisted her best efforts. Once and again she tried, but without success; it was beyond her strength. She could not get out!

"Oh, dear," breathed Janet in dismay.

She tried to force it out sideways. But this was even less practicable if anything. Perceiving finally the nature of her mechanical difficulty, she turned with new hopes to the end that was against the door. As she expected, this proved to be the proper place to take hold; but now the board moved only to make a noise that was amazing. The method of its surprising operation was like the stuttering of a stick when it is rubbed endwise on a box; but as this was a board and as it operated against a rumbly shack, it reverberated like a giant drum; it was an excellent apparatus for making artificial thunder. At her very first effort it gave a little jump and made a noise sufficient to put all the silence on the prairie to flight. She let go at once. More deliberate efforts brought forth results still more tremendous; it was something between a volley and a groan.

Now that she had done what she had, she felt that, embarrassing as it was, she might as well get through with it and show herself promptly. She might as well make the noise all at once as to make it piecemeal.

It was like operating a gatling gun. The board, being sprung down, had a considerable distance to move before it would come free, but Janet, having put her hands to it, stuck to it without flinching. It set the whole shack a-going; those boards made such a noise as they had not made since the day they went through the sawmill in long-drawn agony. But she got it free. Being through with it, she set the board softly in the corner; then she calmed herself and stepped forth.

So far as Janet could see, he considered it the most natural meeting in the world. Jonas Hicks, fortunately, was not easily confused. She lost no time, however, in beginning her explanation.

"You see, Mr. Hicks, I was going on horse-back from Wanger's farm up to the county-seat to take the examination, and just as I was passing here—"

Poor Janet; she had to tell that whole story over again. She told it with particular attention to plausible detail; she wanted him to have a perfect understanding of just how it was.

"Oh, yes—just so—I see," he would say promptly. "You just got lost on the prairie. And you've been stopping a few days with Steve."

As if it were nothing! Such ready belief and general inconsequentiality bothered Janet. She did not know, of course, that Jonas was hardly the sort of a Texan to feel comfortable in having a woman stand before him in the defensive, stating her case. Upon her first appearance he had concealed his surprise and rallied nobly to the courtesies of the occasion; it was sufficient that he was in the presence of the fair. Having heard enough to get the facts of her adventure and grasp her present situation, it was hardly in him to play the part of the unconvinced and give her a hearing through the corroborating details—it was too inquisitorial for him. Suspicion? He would have felt vitally impeached. He could not stand judicially; he would have knocked down the man that did it. For this reason, while he manifested sufficient interest, he escaped from his position by finding casual employment; he examined the skillet, looked into the provision box, and presently set about getting his supper, which, he insisted, he was perfectly capable of doing. Janet persevered with her story. He kept up his interest, making a mere anecdote out of her tale and mitigating the atmosphere with the sound of pots and kettles.

"Well, now; if that don't beat all—Naturally—Just what would happen—" Such was the tenor of his remarks. As if nothing more need really be said.

To Janet, his too ready acceptance was peculiarly unsatisfying.

"And then," he remarked, just as she was coming to it, "I bet you walked right round in a circle."

She wished most heartily that she could have replied, "Oh, no," and explained that that wasn't the way of it at all. She felt that her whole story must seem to him an easily concocted, and a merely necessary fiction. But as that was exactly what did happen she had to accept this part of it from him and do her best with other details. She wished he would pay more strict attention.

"And so," she finally ended, "as Mr. Brown went away just a while ago to get my horse, I was rather frightened when I heard somebody coming. I suppose I surprised you too."

"Well, yes; I must say you did, sort of. But of course when I heard that noise I knew something was bound to come of it. But I managed to save my appetite."

"There isn't very much left to eat," she said seriously.

"Oh, I've got a plenty to eat right there in my wagon. Pie is good enough for anybody. I've got a real Northern pie."

He made a trip to the wagon and came back with the pie. He placed the pie in the middle of the repast and arranged knife and fork on their respective sides of it. Having it properly disposed and everything in readiness he invited her to join him. Janet, because she had had supper, was inclined to refuse. But there is something cordial about a pie's countenance, especially if it be a pie of one's own country, and still more especially if one has been living regularly on *frijole* beans. She cut her regrets short and accepted. It seemed to her, though, that all human companionship was being rather strictly confined to the process of eating.

Plainly he considered her the guest; he took her cup and poured the coffee himself.

"It is a beautiful evening, isn't it," remarked Janet.

"I was just going to say it was a nice night. Quite a flock of stars out."

"A flock, did you say?"

"Well, sort of. I don't usually speak of them that way. Only on special occasions. Hasn't Steve got any sweetenin'?"

He had just rattled the spoon in the sugar bowl and found it empty. Janet was sorry to say that she had poured out the last grain of it that very evening. She explained to him how the lamb had stepped into a bowlful and thus contributed to the present shortage.

"Ain't Steve got a jug of molasses? He ought to have some sweetenin' somewheres."

"Why, I did see a jug of something under the bed. I don't know what is in it, though."

He went to investigate, getting down on the door-sill and entering the shack on his knees. Presently he reappeared, smelling the cork.

"It ain't anything more or less than molasses," he reported.

As he sat down, the off wheeler of the team, which had been drawn up a short distance from the fire, dropped on his paunch with a great rattling of chain and began placidly chewing his cud. Following his example, an ox in the middle of the string got down on his knees and began chewing. At the same moment the lamb, which had fallen out of bed and found his way out of the shack, announced himself with a bleat and went toddling off toward the darkness. Janet jumped up at once and went after him. Having captured him, she brought him back and stowed him comfortably in her lap, drawing the edge of her skirt up over him.

"I suppose you've noticed, Miss Janet," he remarked, as he again turned his attention to the jug, "that the animals out in these parts don't know very much. They make people lots of trouble."

"Oh, I don't mind the trouble at all. You see, I saved this one's life myself; that's why I am so interested in caring for him. He's an orphan."

"So I see. There's liable to be plenty of them. Are you partial to orphans?"

"I could hardly help caring for him. Of course one naturally is."

Jonas again turned his attention to the jug, removing the cork and placing it upside down on the ground. Janet held a saucer to receive her share. The molasses was slow about making its appearance.

"This Golden Drip is a little late about coming. It's as stubborn as old Doc Wharton used to be."

"Was he stubborn?" Janet asked, keeping the saucer level.

"He wasn't much of anything else. He was so stubborn that when he drowned in the Comanche he floated upstream."

"Really?"

"Wasn't any doubt about it. Some people said that his foot must 'a' been caught in the stirrup and the horse dragged him up that far from where he went in. But I always claimed it was just natural."

As the molasses had not yet responded, he up-ended the jug still farther and waited for results.

"I suppose," he queried, "that Steve has told you about things down home. And all about his mother?"

"He told me that he lost his mother last winter."

"Ye-e-e-es," he said reflectively, drawing the word out as a thick sluggish stream began to pile up in the saucer.

When she exclaimed "enough," he lowered the bottom of the jug and kept the mouth over the saucer as the molasses continued to run from it.

"You can't stop that stuff by saying *Wo*," he remarked, whirling the jug in his hands to stop the flow from the lip. "It isn't as thick, though, as some that I've seen."

"No!"

"I don't suppose Steve told you about the molasses I had with the 'J. K.' outfit one winter."

"No, he didn't tell me anything about it."

"Well, that molasses was so thick that when you got too much on a flapjack, all you had to do was to give the jug a few turns and wind the molasses right up into it again. You could wrap it around the neck of the jug till next time if you wanted to. If you'll just excuse me a moment, Miss Janet, I'll put this jug back in home, sweet home, again."

When he had put it where he found it, under the foot of the bed, he returned to his place and passed the flapjacks. He insisted that she try one at least.

"So he told you about his mother. And maybe about his house?"

"He didn't tell me much about his house—just about his mother. He showed me the clipping about her. He didn't tell me anything in particular about her."

"Well, that's all the same. Just the same as if he told you."

Janet sampled the pancake and complimented him upon his cooking, in return for which he told her his recipe, which could be varied with water "according to taste." There came a pause in which Mr. Hicks seemed to be thinking.

"Can you play the piano?" he asked.

"I can play some," answered Janet. "But I am a little out of practice lately."

"You'd soon enough pick that up, as long as you know how."

The first lot of pancakes having dwindled, he got up and put on the remainder of the batter.

As Janet declined his offer of more, he insisted that she start on the pie.

"Are you fond of piano music?" she inquired as he sat down.

"Most any kind suits me. I suppose you can play most any

Charles D. Stewart

kind of a tune."

"Yes, mostly. As I say, I am a little out of practice lately. But my music always comes back to me suddenly after a day or two."

"Steve has a piano," he said.

There came a hiatus in the conversation. Janet applied herself to the pie.

"Mr. Hicks," she said suddenly, "I should think Mr. Brown would hardly choose to come out here and do a sheep-herder's work. Especially as I understand he doesn't really have to."

"Well, it would seem that way, looking at it from this end. It's a little lonesome out here when there isn't anybody around. But down home there isn't anybody around his house, and that's lonesomer still. There a person would notice it; but you don't expect anything else of a shack. I don't suppose he has been on the inside of that house more than once in two or three weeks."

"And yet he lives there?"

"Oh, yes. Gets along good, too, as far as that goes. He washes the dishes on the porch and hangs the pan up outside. I guess he borrowed some of his style from me. Steve would make a pretty good Ranger yet; he hasn't got spoiled. But his ma told him he mustn't ever join them."

"Why," exclaimed Janet, "does *he* think of joining the Rangers?"

"Oh, no—not now. I don't suppose he ever thinks of such an

idea. He's got too many other things to tend to, anyway."

"Then, why should she tell him that?"

"That was just an idea she had. When he was a young fellow about eighteen or nineteen he had an idea of being a Ranger, and he gave her considerable worry, I guess. Steve was like his father was, and she was always watching over him to see that he didn't get into danger. Steve's ma was hardly more than up to his elbow. She looked like a little girl alongside of him. She had real white hair."

"He must have been very fond of his mother."

"Thought as much of her as if he had picked her out himself. But as I was going to tell—Towards the last when she was down sick and pretty near faded out, she seemed to think he wasn't any more than a little boy that had just grown up big. She always did seem to have pretty much that idea anyway; and he never let on but what he was. As long as he fetched and carried for her, and never got into any danger except when he kept it secret, I don't suppose she ever exactly noticed when he did grow up. And when she died you could see that she was worried about what would become of him. I went for the doctor when she died. Steve got out a fast horse and I made some pretty quick time. When I got the doctor to the house I went into the room with him; and you could see she was n 't going to hold out much longer. She seemed to know it too. The last thing she said that night was, 'Good-bye, Stevie; don't go and join the Rangers.'"

"And what did he say?"

"He told her he wouldn't—just as honest as if it was all so. That satisfied her and she shut her eyes again, and that was the way she went. 'Good-bye, Stevie, don't go and join the Rangers.'"

"He didn't usually tell her everything?" said Janet reflectively.

"Not till he saw fit. Old Steve was pretty much the same way. If it was anything she'd worry about, he'd do it first. Then sometime when it was all over, he'd let the cat out of the bag. The old man sort of spoiled her; and Steve just naturally took hold the same way."

"They always did tell her, then?"

"Sooner or later."

"He struck me as a man that was—rather fond of his mother."

"He thought she couldn't be beat. She pretty near run him and old Steve; they were two of a kind. They wouldn't 'a' dared to do anything if she was against it. I guess that was the reason they went ahead on their own hook on anything she might worry about. They were afraid she'd say no, I guess."

"Then she really did have something to say, after all," suggested Janet.

"She twisted them around her finger pretty much as it was. And that's where Steve misses her. He's used to being run. He's lost. About a week after she was buried he took her picture down out of the parlor and hung it up nearer the kitchen where he could see it every day."

"But," exclaimed Janet, "I thought you said he hardly ever went into the house!"

Jonas took a moment for consideration. Then he put his hand to his hip pocket and felt around in it. Not finding what he was looking for, and being evidently at a loss, he cast his eyes about on the vacant ground. Presently his eye lit on Janet's yellow oil-coat. He reached out and took it, and having folded it somewhat like a cushion, so that its back presented a smooth surface, he again made search of his various pockets. When he had hunted down the elusive lead-pencil he moistened it on his tongue and set to work deliberately to draw on the slicker. The result of his work was simply a square.

"That," he said, "is Steve's house."

Moistening the pencil again, he drew another square, somewhat smaller, so that it just touched the other square corner to corner.

"That's the kitchen," he explained.

Again he drew a square; this one touching corners with the kitchen so that it faced the side of the house.

"That's the milk-house," he said.

The three squares, one large and two smaller ones, being thus joined at the corners, made a space between them. This space, surrounded on but three sides, seemed to be open towards the road.

"Now, this place in between here," began Jonas, "is out of doors. But it ain't really out of doors at all, because it has got a roof on it and has a floor. It ain't a room exactly nor it ain't a porch. It's a sort of an inside porch or an outside room. Now, the open side of this place faces the road; but it isn't open to the road at all, because there is a lattice-work there

Charles D. Stewart

covered with vines. This lattice"—he wet the pencil and set it to work again—"this lattice that closes this place runs out from the side of the house, but it doesn't join to the corner of the milk-house, because you see that would close this place all up so that you couldn't come in from outside. It comes a distance away from the corner of the milk-house; and that makes a door so that you can go out into the yard without going through the kitchen. So you see, you can go into this inside place without going through the house at all."

Janet drew closer, the better to study the plan.

"Yes; I see how that is," she said.

"Well, now," he continued, "these three parts of the house have each got a door opening into this inside place—the dining-room door, and the kitchen door, and the milk-house door. And right here beside the dining-room door is a bench where Steve washes up, and a looking-glass. And right on the other side of this door is where he hung her picture. That's how it is that he hardly ever goes into the house at all and he's got her picture right in there where he does his work. He cooks some in Aunt Lucy's kitchen, and eats and sets here. Aunt Lucy has got a new place to work."

"I understand perfectly well now what you meant, Mr. Hicks. It is perfectly plain."

She had rather awkwardly accused him of getting his tale tangled; and now that he suddenly brought the whole weight of this explanation to bear upon the point at issue, she felt a new striking-in of her shame. She hoped that if there was to be any further explanation it would not be in this particular connection.

"Now," said Jonas, wetting his pencil and setting to work on the interior of the house, "right here in the main house is a long dining-room. And a hall runs from this dining-room right straight through onto the front porch. You can set right here at the head of the table and eat and see everything that is passing on the road. And there is a cool draught right through. Off to the right of this hall is the parlor."

Jonas wetted the pencil unusually and worked it busily in the corner of the parlor till he had made a very black and shiny little square. Janet leaned farther over to watch him.

"And this here," he announced, "is the piano."

Janet resumed her erect position.

"It is a very convenient house in some ways," she said. "It has certain advantages for a warm climate."

"It's all figured out," said Jonas.

He made a dot by holding the pencil straight down and twirling it round. This was about the middle of the "inside place." Janet leaned over and became interested again.

"Now," he continued, "suppose it is a rainy day. Right here in the middle of this inside place is a chain pump. You don't have to go outside for anything. Or suppose it is a hot day. And maybe there is a big company dinner to get. You can set here by the lattice where it is cool and breezy,—the Gulf breeze comes right in that place by the milk-house,—and keep track of what's going on in the kitchen. You don't have to go right into the kitchen once in a week if you don't want to. But it's a good thing to keep an eye on Aunt Lucy or the best of them. They're likely to hand out half of the provisions to the rest of the niggers. You see it's fixed so that it don't make any difference whether it's rainy or hot, or whether you've got company clothes on or not. You can set right here with your knitting and see into the kitchen or out to the road —but people going past on the road can't see you."

"It is an outside kitchen without the disadvantages of a separate building, isn't it! And it looks like a part of the house, too."

"So does the milk-house. When you come out of the side door of the dining-room the milkhouse is right in front of you. And to your right is the kitchen door. Everything's handy. Old Steve used to be a great hand for company. And I guess Steve B. is likely to turn out just as bad. So you see these are all three joined at the corners and this place between is all floored and roofed over, and there is a lattice and vines where you can see out onto the road. And it's nice and cool. You can set right here in the shade and tend to everything."

Having submitted the plans to her contemplation awhile Jonas withdrew the slicker as if he were considering any possible improvements.

Janet, being tired by her constrained position in viewing the work,—for she had not moved entirely round to his side of the supper,—straightened up and spent the interval in a new survey of the stars. It rested her neck. As on the previous nights it was clear and spacious. There were stars and stars. The biggest and brightest stood out in unison; in between them and hanging far off in space were so many others that all confusion seemed straightened out in the unity of the infinite. It was all very beautiful—heaven is not disorder, after all. And yet a coyote, complaining in the distance, seemed to set the world to a false note. Her mind seemed tangled in light as her eye, following the stars, was led along the devious invisible lines from one to another. She had a feeling as if she would like to look up the definition of "you" in the dictionary.

When she came back to earth again, Jonas was sitting there awaiting her return. One would almost think he was waiting for an answer.

Janet looked at her watch. It was twenty minutes after ten—but she did not know whether it was right or not.

"I hope I haven't been keeping you up, Miss Janet," said Jonas. "Whenever your time comes to turn in, go right along. Don't consider me company."

"Oh, it wasn't that; I was just wondering what time it is. Do you suppose, Mr. Hicks, that he will have any difficulty finding that horse and getting it back here? I should think he would get lost."

"How long has he been gone?"

"A little over an hour."

"Oh, that ain't bad. You can't lose Steve."

"No, of course not. I thought it was longer."

"What time is it?"

"Twenty minutes after ten by my watch. But I don't really know what time it is."

"Well, there ain't much use knowin'. Time is queer anyway on a prairie. Sometimes it takes a considerable while for it to go past. And then again, as the other fellow said, 'Time is shorter than it is long.' Maybe if you are sleepy you'd better go to bed."

"Well—I believe I will. I don't suppose I had better wait any longer. Will you find a place to sleep? Maybe you will want to use my slicker."

"Oh, I'm all right. I'll just chase away these cattle and roll in under the wagon. And if you should hear me serrynadin' you with a horse-fiddle after a while, don't be scared. That's me snoring. I'm what they call a sound sleeper."

"Good-night, Mr. Hicks."

"Same to you, Miss Janet."

CHAPTER XI

The sun, lifting his countenance above the horizon that morning, centred his whole attention upon a pair of polished brass-bound hubs. The rest of the scene, grass and flowers "in unrespective same," formed a mere background on the general plane of existence while the sun beamed upon the brass—delighted, no doubt, to find an affinity in this unexpected place.

We accentuate the detail slightly, our reason being that Janet, whenever she had occasion to tell how it all happened, was sure to make mention of the brass hubs. Unconscious as she may have been of it at the time, the hubs commanded the scene and formed the shining high-light of memory's picture; and as the years passed they took on a still brighter polish.

The hubs belonged to a snug-looking Rockaway buggy. Hitched to the buggy was her own horse, which was tied to a post of the corral. The gate of the corral was open and the sheep were gone. Jonas's outfit was gone too; there was nobody in sight.

As she stood looking and wondering, Steve emerged from the gully; and having saluted her in his usual manner he began to explain to her how the change was wrought. When he returned late that night and found that Jonas Hicks was in

Charles D. Stewart

charge, he saw his way clear to solve her transportation problems. As a horse without a saddle would hardly do for her, he remounted and rode almost to town on the main road, where he borrowed a buggy. Getting back again he found that the much-expected herder had put in his appearance with a man to help him; the two were now out with the sheep. The wagon had not arrived because the bed with sheep-stalls was out of repair; a second helper would come with it later in the day and in the meantime Jonas would follow the flock with his wagon and two yoke of oxen.

As to Mr. Pete Harding, that delinquent, instead of being conscience-smitten by his long absence, had returned as one who is the bearer of glad tidings, the burden of his song being that he had been most surpassingly drunk. Steve, taking into consideration that the man, being now satisfied with his achievements and the proud possessor of a headache, would settle down to the simple life with all the more interest, let him off without a word of reproof. And besides, Mr. Brown, though he did not say so, was grateful to the man for having stayed away as long as he did.

Thus Steve Brown was free to do as he pleased. He would himself take Janet to her destination at the county-seat; and if she would allow him to,—he seemed to lose all his usual self-confidence at this point in his relations toward her,—he would wait there until she had taken the examination. And then, if she were willing, he would take her wherever she wished to go. Janet, protesting mildly against putting him to so much trouble, accepted the offer.

"That's the best thing for us to do," he said.

So it was decided; and when breakfast was over and the hieroglyphic oil-coat had been stowed under the seat of the buggy, Janet's horse got the word to go.

Not without regret, nor certain light allusions to the state other feelings, did Janet part company with the shack and the now familiar prairie. The shack had been a house to her, and one whose roof and walls had held her in the very closest relations; and besides, though she did not say a word about this, it was the only residence she had ever met which she could possibly imagine herself saving up enough money to buy. This was one of its secrets.

Steve, taking a route of his own, drove twice through the waters of the wandering Comanche. At these wide shallows, Janet's gossip ceased while she held to his coat-sleeve and kept her eye on the water as it hurried through the spokes and rose steadily to the hub. But when the stout pony pulled them up the opposite bank and the road lay before them the same length as before, she again took up the thread of the conversation. As everybody knows, a conversation can lead almost anywhere; the talk will get to wherever it is going by some route as long as words point the way, and always the story of one's *self* will leak through the sentences in the end. And where is there anything so conducive to the objects of conversation as a Rockaway buggy wheeling it over the cushioned sward and the flowers trooping by? We are not going to intrude upon their pleasant situation; suffice it to say that as time passed he became more and more Steve Brown and she became increasingly Janet.

It was about the middle of the forenoon when they reached Belleville, the prairie highway becoming now a shady homestead street, with Southern cottages ensconced in vines and shrubbery and sheltered by prosperous trees. Presently they turned into a street of stores which delivered them finally to a hitching-rack at the end of a walk leading up to the steps of the court-house.

The Professor, it devolved upon inquiry, was busy just at

Charles D. Stewart

present, but if the young lady would step up to his room he would give her an examination shortly. Steve, being thus left to himself, went outside again. At the side of the gravel walk was a green bench presided over by a china-berry tree; he sat down here and waited. Occasionally a passer-by diversified the tenor of his waiting—now a straight-paced lawyer garbed in black and thinking dark thoughts; again, a leisurely stockman arrayed like himself with sombrero and spurs. His own spurs he had not thought to remove since he got back that morning. The little town, like other county capitals, had an atmosphere that was half the hush of the court-room and partly the quiet of academic groves, in which state of being the inhabitants were peacefully and permanently established, the court-house being, in truth, Belleville's principal industry.

Having nodded to several and encountered none that he was well acquainted with, he arose and went into the court-house again. After a spell of indecision in the corridor, he turned and proceeded up the dark-banistered stairs to the second story. At the head of the stairs was a long hall with two rows of doors and a window at each end. One of the farther doors was open, but gave forth no sound. In this direction he turned his steps,—ostensibly toward the window which was invitingly open,—and as he passed the door he turned his head and viewed the scene of the "examination." The place was filled with cast-iron desks screwed to the floor and surrounded by blackboards; and all empty except for the seat which held Janet. The Professor, elevated on a little platform with a table before him, sat sidewise in his chair out of regard to a set of questions which he had chalked upon the blackboard; meanwhile he tapped the table with his finger-nails and regarded Janet with a look of great profundity. It was a speechless process; he wrote the questions on the blackboard, she wrote the answers on the paper. Janet, evidently perplexed, bit the end of her penholder. She turned her eyes to the door as Steve passed and gave him a furtive look. It made him feel as if he were a boy again and Janet a little girl being kept after school.

He passed onward to the window. Below him was a view of the court-house yard, and through the trees a glimpse of the short business street. For a little while he made this the object of his attention, then he turned about and proceeded to the window at the other end. As he passed the door he turned his eyes again and took quick survey of affairs inside the examination-room, The other window, being at the back of the courthouse, opened upon a wide prospect; in the near distance were tree-hidden cottages, beyond this scene was the stretch of prairie again. Steve sat down on the sill to wait. But in a little while he got up and went back to the first window. When he passed the door again the young lady blushed.

Janet was now in the very midst of that dread ordeal known as a "test." She was being tried for her life,—which is to say her living,—and her speechless inquisitor made the most of his attainments. "Give the source and course of the Volga." Having writ down that cold-blooded query he ascended his dais again and suppressed all feelings of triumph. Janet again put the pen-holder to her teeth. Evidently this was more than the young lady was able to "give." He drummed on the wood with his finger-nails; otherwise he sat before her like patience on a pedestal. His single spectator, feeling herself no match for such a brain, was beginning to abandon all hope of passing.

Steve Brown, having gathered some inkling of Janet's mental troubles, was beginning to have his opinion of the whole procedure. Seeing her in such difficulty he had a feeling of revolt against educational things in general, but as the wrong seemed to be beyond his individual powers to remedy, he

Charles D. Stewart

could only make another trip to the end of the hall. Glancing again at the questions on the board he looked in vain for some inquiry upon the subject of Climate. There did not seem to be even one. And when next he came back, after composing himself for about half a minute on the window ledge, the door was unceremoniously shut in his face!

He had come to a definite stop in hope of finding at least one question upon the subject of Climate; the door was shut in his face. Confronting him was the printed legend—"County Superintendent." His heels were frozen to the floor. If it had not been that it was an improper and very unusual thing to do, he could have shot each particular letter of that announcement full of bullet holes.

The remedy for this peculiar outrage not at once presenting itself, he turned on his heel and made another trip to the farther window where he at once came face-about and began patrolling the hallway, past the door and back again, his spurs clicking sharply and his high boot-heels punctuating his progress as if every step put a period to his thoughts.

As he thus took his mind a-walking, everything about Janet's present situation struck him in a light more obnoxious and foolish. Examination! Examin*ation*! The idea of that girl having to go to that fellow to be tested! The idea of *his* having any such *authority* over her! And besides, if that little Professor really wanted to get an idea of her merits, why didn't he talk to her and find out whether she had common sense? She certainly had more than *he* had. As if any man with half an eye couldn't see that she was the very person to teach children!

As Janet's situation struck him more deeply, and he began to realize how she might feel if she failed, he stopped and glared again at that brazen lettering. Possibly she was failing now. He felt that if he had the authority, or any proper cause,—which he could hardly make out that he had,—he would march in and reform the thing right then and there. But he had no authority. The other fellow had the authority. And the right to close the door between them! This being actually the case he whirled about and resumed his marching back and forth; and his spurs began snapping their jaws again.

Janet, when she saw the door shut, caught her breath and paid strict attention to the paper. The examiner, evidently unconscious of anything but his own precise self, went officially to the blackboard and took up next the writing of another set of questions. He wrote impromptu and with considerable readiness, pausing occasionally to think up a poser.

Regularly she heard her escort coming down the hall on his return trip, and each time she suspended mental operations until he was safely away again. About the time that she had done her best, and worst, to the subject of Geography, he failed to pass the door; his footsteps seemed to turn with a new and lighter expression in some other direction. Then she heard no more of him.

The next subject was Grammar. She caught glimpses of the questions as her examiner walked back and forth from one end of a sentence to the other. As grammar is a subject in which there is some limit to the number of possible questions, she felt that she now had an advantage. She would now do wonders providing he did not ask her something easy.

Luckily he did not. She pushed Geography aside and took a new sheet of foolscap with every prospect of passing. At first it had looked very much as if she were going to fail.

Steve's withdrawal had merely been due to the sudden

realization that he was making a great deal of noise in the court-house; whereupon he saw that, all things considered, he could contain himself better somewhere else. He went down the stairs, through the corridor, and out of the grounds. Thence his feet carried him clean to the other side of town.

When he found himself upon the silent shore of the prairie he turned about with the intention of going straight back, but he was three times delayed, first at the hitching-rack in front of "Hart's General Store," where a knot of story-tellers halted him to tell him about the phenomenal good time of his herder, and again in front of the post-office, where another group of loiterers had to be listened to; and finally, having made his escape when he felt that it was high time to go, he had the bad luck to run into Judge Tillotson, whose propensity to talk was such that he could not be denied a hearing without good excuse.

When he at last arrived at the foot of the court-house path, he saw Janet sitting on the bench under the china-berry tree. How long had she been waiting for him? As she caught sight of him she began dabbing her eyes hastily with her handkerchief. Steve saw this. His stride lengthened as he came up the path. Having reached the bench he dropped down suddenly beside her, his arm extended along the top of the bench at her back.

"How did you make out, Miss Janet?"

There was a lugubrious attempt at a smile as she turned her eyes toward him. The tears had been put into her pocket; but still he could see that her eyes were swimming. To him they looked more wonderfully gentle, more wholly true than any eyes he had ever seen.

"Well—Mr. Brown—I failed," she said.

"What! Didn't he let you pass?"

"I already had a third-class certificate, you know."

"Yes; but that isn't any good to you."

"No," she said meditatively. "Even second-class would have got me that school near Merrill. I think I would have passed, too, if he had only been fair in Geography and History."

"What? Did he do anything that wasn't on the square?" he asked sternly.

"Oh, I didn't mean it that way. It is always possible to be unfair in Geography and History, you know,—and besides there is a good deal of luck about it, too. He said he would have let me pass, but he had decided to raise the standard."

She felt his arm stiffen behind her like an iron bar. She thought he was going to rise.

"But he was *perfectly* fair," she added quickly.

Steve's muscle relaxed slowly; he resumed his former lax attitude and fell to thinking.

"You deserve to get a certificate and you *didn't*," he said, suddenly sitting up again. "It isn't *right*."

This last word came out as sharp as a challenge to fight. He seemed to have stiffened up in the saddle with the straight look of indomitable will. Janet's eyes opened wider with the impression she got of him.

"Oh, it isn't a great matter—except that—of course—it is a little disappointing."

"Yes. And somebody that it doesn't make any difference about will come along and pass." His eye still had fight in it. "You like Texas?" he said suddenly. "Don't you think it is a pretty good state?"

"Oh, yes, indeed," answered Janet. "I was very much in hope of being able to stay. If I had only had more time to study—more time—"

There was a quaver in her voice, and she let the sentence end itself there.

He sat for a moment looking straight at the middle of the path before him. Then deliberately he turned about, put his arm behind her again, and took her hand in his.

"Janet," he said, "if you had been here in two or three months from now, there was a question I had all made up to ask you."

"A question?"

"As long as you might have to go away, I might as well tell you now—before you are gone. I was going to ask you in two or three months whether, if—But no. That isn't fair. What I mean is, *will* you marry me? Would you?"

Janet paused during a space that would best be represented by a musical rest—a silence in the midst of a symphony. Then her clear eyes turned toward him.

"Yes, Steve; I would."

"You would! Do you mean that *now*—for keeps?"

"I could go and live with you anywhere in the world. I could *almost* have answered that two days ago."

Her hand was taken tighter in his grasp. The edge of his sombrero touched the top of her head, and she felt herself being taken under its broad brim with a sense of everlasting shelter. And just then they were interrupted. A visitor to the court-room came up the path—unnoticed till he was almost past. At the same time there was a sound of footsteps coming down the courthouse steps. It was the Professor. Seeing which Steve released her hand and assumed a more conventional public attitude until this particular spectator should be gone. The Professor passed. He kept on his way down the path and did not look back; whereupon Steve took possession of her hand again. It was such a fine delicate hand to him—so small and tender a hand to have to grapple with things of this rough world; he looked at it thoughtfully and hefted it as so much precious property in his own.

"I am mighty glad you said that," he offered. "I was afraid you might have to leave. That's why I wanted you to pass."

"And that's why I *wanted* to pass, too," she said.

Now that the coast was clear they resumed their confessions. At times they sat in silence, holding hands.

As the time approached when they ought to start back, they were reminded to make more definite plans. He would take her to Merrill, leave the horse and buggy there, and come home to Thornton on the night train. On the following day he would come down with one of his own horses to get the buggy and she could ride up "home" with him and catch the early train back.

"I want you to come up right away and look over the house and get acquainted with the neighborhood."

"Are we going to have nice neighbors?" she asked.

"First-class. A mighty fine lot of folks. They'll all put themselves out to accommodate you. I think you'll like them."

"Oh, I know I shall," she answered.

"And I'll have something I want to give you, too. And we can talk things over and make up our minds about the date. I don't see any use in waiting a long time, do you?"

"Well—no; not too long. But of course there are quite a number of things that need to be done first."

"Yes—of course," he mused. "Quite a number of things that have to be done. And there's the license to get, too," looking up suddenly at the court-house.

"What!—right now?"

"We might as well get it while we're right here, don't you think? I might have to come out here after it anyway—and maybe the Comanche would be up and on a rampage. Here we are right now. And there's the court-house."

"It does seem the most sensible way—of course. You had better do whatever you think best."

Upon receiving this commission he arose and proceeded for the license. As he set foot upon the court-house steps he paused and looked back at her. He was straight as a ramrod; there was self-confidence in his carriage and pride in his mien.

"I'll bet ten dollars *I'll* pass," he said.

CHAPTER XII

Susie's ma—she who made the "real Northern" pie—was busy in her kitchen. A dishpanful of dough, which had risen till it overhung the edges of the pan, indicated that it was high time to knead a batch of bread. She was just clearing the table with this end in view when she heard a familiar sound in the distance, and going to the window she saw that Jonas Hicks was at home again. He turned loose his "string," now reduced to two yoke, and went into the house.

While it was no unusual thing for Jonas to go into the house, it was seldom that he stayed long, for which reason Mrs. Berry tarried at the window in expectation of getting another sight of him. While she was thus waiting she saw Mrs. Harmon making her way across the open. Evidently she was bound for Jonas's house. She had hardly reached the door when Mrs. Norton and Kitty Wright made their appearance on Claxton Road, arm in arm. They turned off the road and bent their steps in the same direction. In a little while Mrs. Plympton and another of her aristocratic neighbors issued forth and joined company, walking faster. They too struck out across the common. What might this mean?

To Mrs. Berry, who knew nothing of the unreturned rockery, and nothing of the mysterious doings of Steve Brown, this was a question which called for an answer.

Charles D. Stewart

Evidently it was no preconcerted move. Mrs. Berry, being a woman, could see, from various indications of dress and manner, that each of them was going simply because she had seen the other do so, and this was reason enough; but still, behind it all, there must have been some original reason; and what was it?

Mrs. Berry proceeded to the kitchen and faced her work. She addressed her remarks particularly to the dough.

"Well, I guess I can just let my work go for *once* in my life," she said. She spread out her hands and pushed down the dough till it was about half its former size. "There, now," she said. "Rise again."

Donning a clean apron and her best hat, and giving Susan some parting instructions, she opened the door and set forth for the common destination. Mrs. Berry had the courage of her curiosity. She was not meddlesome, but only interested; and as there was nothing whatever between her and what she saw in the world,—not even an education,—she dealt with life in her own resourceful way. Mrs. Berry was a "railroad widow"; she supported herself and Susan by ceaseless industry helped out by a small income received from "the Company" when her husband was killed in the faithful discharge of his duty.

By the time she had put in her appearance at Jonas's ever-open door, the ladies had come to a period in their conference with Jonas and now they were engaged in expressing various sorts of surprise. They were quite astonished at something—whatever the nature of it might be.

"Yes, she had on that kind of a hat," Jonas was saying. "But she ain't any woman from around here. She is a school-teacher and educated. I know her."

There was another chorus of "I declare!" which came to a stop as Mrs. Berry rapped on the door-jamb; then all reference to their business was dropped as they welcomed her in and made the usual polite inquiries regarding herself and little Susan. Mrs. Berry seated herself in the proffered chair without any reference to what the nature of her own errand might have been. When it was seen that she had settled down to stay, Mrs. Harmon took in hand to make everything plain and open. They had just received news that Mr. Brown was engaged to be married. It was this, Mrs. Harmon explained, that they had all been talking over, and they were all very much delighted. Mrs. Berry, on her part, was not a whit less interested in such things than the rest of them; she expressed her opinion that it was really the best thing for a man to do. With which sentiment they all agreed. Then Jonas spoke.

"You see, Mrs. Berry," he said, "Steve and the young lady passed me on the road coming in from the ranch; and they stopped and told me all about it. They just got engaged to-day."

"Oh, indeed," said Mrs. Berry. And then she created consternation by a most embarrassing question. "And were you all expecting it?"

"Well—yes. We rather *suspected* it, you know," put in Mrs. Harmon, viewing her benignly. "We heard in a roundabout way that Mr. Brown was paying attention to a young lady."

This crisis safely passed, gossip revived and took on new life, in the course of which Mrs. Berry gathered a few details regarding the bride-elect. Talk had not proceeded far, however, when Mrs. Harmon rose and stationed herself behind Jonas's kitchen table.

"Ladies," she said, "I think that, just at this time, and while we are all together, we had better call a meeting of the Circle." She took up Jonas's long-handled batter-spoon and rapped three times on the table. The result was that they all sat up a little straighter and came to order. "As you are all aware," she continued, "the business of our last meeting was left in a rather unfinished and unsatisfactory state. It has just occurred to me that there is a little point that ought to be taken up promptly and brought to a general understanding. I would suggest that anything in our last meeting which might be of a—Star Chamber nature—be expunged from the records, verbal and otherwise. In every sense I mean— entirely. Will some one make a motion to that effect?"

Kitty Wright arose to the occasion.

"I move," she said, "that the proceedings of the last meeting be expunged. And that it be understood that it be considered a permanent meeting of the committee of the whole behind closed doors. Also that it be understood that any member— such as Mrs. Plympton, for instance—is entitled to vote now, and make inquiries from any of her sisters, at any time, regarding the nature of the present parliamentary vocabulary."

"Second the motion," said Mrs. Plympton.

"Moved and seconded that the last meeting be of the aforesaid nature."

The motion was carried.

"And now," said Mrs. Harmon, rapping again with the spoon, "as this little matter is tended to, I think it no more than proper, in view of the pleasant news we have just received, that we turn our attention, while the opportunity offers, to an *entirely different* matter." Here she turned a wary glance in the direction of the much-mystified Mrs. Berry. "While we are all here I think it would be a matter of pleasure to all concerned that we make some plans for the proper treatment of the young lady who is going to settle among us. Possibly we could do something to entertain her and make her feel at home. If any of you have an idea on which we could act, motions to that effect will now be in order."

"Mrs. President," said Kitty Wright, rising to her feet, "I think that would be just lovely. I move that when Miss Smith arrives to-morrow she be invited to a chicken dinner at the home of our worthy President; and that two members of the Circle be invited, including myself."

"Second the motion," said Mrs. Norton.

"Moved and seconded that the young lady and her escort be invited to dinner at the home of the President, and that Mrs. Wright and Mrs. Norton include themselves. Are you ready for the question?"

"Question."

The motion was carried.

"Mrs. President," said Mrs. Plympton, rising and receiving recognition, "I understand from the information that has been conveyed to us by Mr. Hicks, that the wedding is not likely to be put off to a very late day. It may occur very soon; therefore any plans that we may have in that regard ought to be set in motion at once. Now, I have just been thinking that I have those fifty Japanese lanterns which we used in the lawn festival. I move that a committee be appointed, at the pleasure of the President, to begin arrangements for celebrating the return of the bridal couple with a reception *al fresco* in our peach orchard. And that the Colonel be notified to have his barn in readiness for another dance."

The motion was seconded and carried by extra unanimous vote.

Mrs. Harmon paused a moment before bringing the meeting to an end. While she was hesitating a chair scraped behind her and Mrs. Berry took the floor.

"I don't know as I belong to this here Circle," said Mrs. Berry, "but anyway I guess I belong to the Square." A murmur of approval showed that they appreciated this view, referring as it did to that rectangular neighborhood surrounding Jonas's twenty acres. "I guess I belong to the Square. And I have just been thinking that as long as Mr. Brown has been living alone around that house he has probably got it into a pretty bad mess. Most likely the kitchen is a sight and the place is all out of order. Somebody ought to go over and sweep and dust and scrub and red things up. If the young lady was to come along to-morrow and see things like that she would think we was a *pretty* sort of a neighborhood. I move and second that I go and do it."

Without a dissenting vote, this motion was carried.

Mrs. Harmon was about to declare the meeting adjourned; but she paused with her spoon in the air. "Mr. Hicks," she said, turning her head in his direction, "I believe you understand about the rockery?"

"Yes," replied Jonas, rising. "I'll tend to that all right. I'll get them back and fixed just the same as before. And as long as everybody is bearing witness, I might as well do the same, as the cat said when she got caught in the mousetrap. Most

The Wrong Woman 199

likely, if Steve has been hauling things around in that house, there will be lots of heavy lifting and tall reaching that needs to be done; so if Mrs. Berry is going over there to fix up I guess I'll go along too."

Upon this the batter-spoon came down and the meeting was declared adjourned. But though it was adjourned, it did not immediately disperse—women's meetings seldom do. Such delightful duties being in the air, they had to be dwelt upon and enlarged, and Jonas had to bring forth further details of his favorable impressions of the young lady. And did he do her justice? Did he let them understand how well-bred and refined and good-looking she was? Did he, in short, convey the information that she was just about the sweetest and most delightful and charming young lady that ever set foot on the soil of Texas? I think, dear reader, that we may safely intrust that duty to Mr. Jonas Hicks.

Charles D. Stewart

Choose from Thousands of 1stWorldLibrary Classics By

A. M. Barnard
Ada Leverson
Adolphus William Ward
Aesop
Agatha Christie
Alexander Aaronsohn
Alexander Kielland
Alexandre Dumas
Alfred Gatty
Alfred Ollivant
Alice Duer Miller
Alice Turner Curtis
Alice Dunbar
Allen Chapman
Alleyne Ireland
Ambrose Bierce
Amelia E. Barr
Amory H. Bradford
Andrew Lang
Andrew McFarland Davis
Andy Adams
Angela Brazil
Anna Alice Chapin
Anna Sewell
Annie Besant
Annie Hamilton Donnell
Annie Payson Call
Annie Roe Carr
Annonaymous
Anton Chekhov
Archibald Lee Fletcher
Arnold Bennett
Arthur C. Benson
Arthur Conan Doyle
Arthur M. Winfield
Arthur Ransome
Arthur Schnitzler
Arthur Train
Atticus
B.H. Baden-Powell
B. M. Bower
B. C. Chatterjee
Baroness Emmuska Orczy
Baroness Orczy
Basil King
Bayard Taylor
Ben Macomber
Bertha Muzzy Bower
Bjornstjerne Bjornson

Booth Tarkington
Boyd Cable
Bram Stoker
C. Collodi
C. E. Orr
C. M. Ingleby
Carolyn Wells
Catherine Parr Traill
Charles A. Eastman
Charles Amory Beach
Charles Dickens
Charles Dudley Warner
Charles Farrar Browne
Charles Ives
Charles Kingsley
Charles Klein
Charles Hanson Towne
Charles Lathrop Pack
Charles Romyn Dake
Charles Whibley
Charles Willing Beale
Charlotte M. Braeme
Charlotte M. Yonge
Charlotte Perkins Stetson
Clair W. Hayes
Clarence Day Jr.
Clarence E. Mulford
Clemence Housman
Confucius
Coningsby Dawson
Cornelis DeWitt Wilcox
Cyril Burleigh
D. H. Lawrence
Daniel Defoe
David Garnett
Dinah Craik
Don Carlos Janes
Donald Keyhoe
Dorothy Kilner
Dougan Clark
Douglas Fairbanks
E. Nesbit
E. P. Roe
E. Phillips Oppenheim
E. S. Brooks
Earl Barnes
Edgar Rice Burroughs
Edith Van Dyne
Edith Wharton

Edward Everett Hale
Edward J. O'Biren
Edward S. Ellis
Edwin L. Arnold
Eleanor Atkins
Eleanor Hallowell Abbott
Eliot Gregory
Elizabeth Gaskell
Elizabeth McCracken
Elizabeth Von Arnim
Ellem Key
Emerson Hough
Emilie F. Carlen
Emily Bronte
Emily Dickinson
Enid Bagnold
Enilor Macartney Lane
Erasmus W. Jones
Ernie Howard Pie
Ethel May Dell
Ethel Turner
Ethel Watts Mumford
Eugene Sue
Eugenie Foa
Eugene Wood
Eustace Hale Ball
Evelyn Everett-green
Everard Cotes
F. H. Cheley
F. J. Cross
F. Marion Crawford
Fannie E. Newberry
Federick Austin Ogg
Ferdinand Ossendowski
Fergus Hume
Florence A. Kilpatrick
Fremont B. Deering
Francis Bacon
Francis Darwin
Frances Hodgson Burnett
Frances Parkinson Keyes
Frank Gee Patchin
Frank Harris
Frank Jewett Mather
Frank L. Packard
Frank V. Webster
Frederic Stewart Isham
Frederick Trevor Hill
Frederick Winslow Taylor

Friedrich Kerst	Hayden Carruth	James Branch Cabell
Friedrich Nietzsche	Helent Hunt Jackson	James DeMille
Fyodor Dostoyevsky	Helen Nicolay	James Joyce
G.A. Henty	Hendrik Conscience	James Lane Allen
G.K. Chesterton	Hendy David Thoreau	James Lane Allen
Gabrielle E. Jackson	Henri Barbusse	James Oliver Curwood
Garrett P. Serviss	Henrik Ibsen	James Oppenheim
Gaston Leroux	Henry Adams	James Otis
George A. Warren	Henry Ford	James R. Driscoll
George Ade	Henry Frost	Jane Abbott
Geroge Bernard Shaw	Henry James	Jane Austen
George Cary Eggleston	Henry Jones Ford	Jane L. Stewart
George Durston	Henry Seton Merriman	Janet Aldridge
George Ebers	Henry W Longfellow	Jens Peter Jacobsen
George Eliot	Herbert A. Giles	Jerome K. Jerome
George Gissing	Herbert Carter	Jessie Graham Flower
George MacDonald	Herbert N. Casson	John Buchan
George Meredith	Herman Hesse	John Burroughs
George Orwell	Hildegard G. Frey	John Cournos
George Sylvester Viereck	Homer	John F. Kennedy
George Tucker	Honore De Balzac	John Gay
George W. Cable	Horace B. Day	John Glasworthy
George Wharton James	Horace Walpole	John Habberton
Gertrude Atherton	Horatio Alger Jr.	John Joy Bell
Gordon Casserly	Howard Pyle	John Kendrick Bangs
Grace E. King	Howard R. Garis	John Milton
Grace Gallatin	Hugh Lofting	John Philip Sousa
Grace Greenwood	Hugh Walpole	John Taintor Foote
Grant Allen	Humphry Ward	Jonas Lauritz Idemil Lie
Guillermo A. Sherwell	Ian Maclaren	Jonathan Swift
Gulielma Zollinger	Inez Haynes Gillmore	Joseph A. Altsheler
Gustav Flaubert	Irving Bacheller	Joseph Carey
H. A. Cody	Isabel Cecilia Williams	Joseph Conrad
H. B. Irving	Isabel Hornibrook	Joseph E. Badger Jr
H. C. Bailey	Israel Abrahams	Joseph Hergesheimer
H. G. Wells	Ivan Turgenev	Joseph Jacobs
H. H. Munro	J. G.Austin	Jules Vernes
H. Irving Hancock	J. Henri Fabre	Julian Hawthrone
H. R. Naylor	J. M. Barrie	Julie A Lippmann
H. Rider Haggard	J. M. Walsh	Justin Huntly McCarthy
H. W. C. Davis	J. Macdonald Oxley	Kakuzo Okakura
Haldeman Julius	J. R. Miller	Karle Wilson Baker
Hall Caine	J. S. Fletcher	Kate Chopin
Hamilton Wright Mabie	J. S. Knowles	Kenneth Grahame
Hans Christian Andersen	J. Storer Clouston	Kenneth McGaffey
Harold Avery	J. W. Duffield	Kate Langley Bosher
Harold McGrath	Jack London	Kate Langley Bosher
Harriet Beecher Stowe	Jacob Abbott	Katherine Cecil Thurston
Harry Castlemon	James Allen	Katherine Stokes
Harry Coghill	James Andrews	L. A. Abbot
Harry Houidini	James Baldwin	L. T. Meade

L. Frank Baum
Latta Griswold
Laura Dent Crane
Laura Lee Hope
Laurence Housman
Lawrence Beasley
Leo Tolstoy
Leonid Andreyev
Lewis Carroll
Lewis Sperry Chafer
Lilian Bell
Lloyd Osbourne
Louis Hughes
Louis Joseph Vance
Louis Tracy
Louisa May Alcott
Lucy Fitch Perkins
Lucy Maud Montgomery
Luther Benson
Lydia Miller Middleton
Lyndon Orr
M. Corvus
M. H. Adams
Margaret E. Sangster
Margret Howth
Margaret Vandercook
Margaret W. Hungerford
Margret Penrose
Maria Edgeworth
Maria Thompson Daviess
Mariano Azuela
Marion Polk Angellotti
Mark Overton
Mark Twain
Mary Austin
Mary Catherine Crowley
Mary Cole
Mary Hastings Bradley
Mary Roberts Rinehart
Mary Rowlandson
M. Wollstonecraft Shelley
Maud Lindsay
Max Beerbohm
Myra Kelly
Nathaniel Hawthrone
Nicolo Machiavelli
O. F. Walton
Oscar Wilde
Owen Johnson
P.G. Wodehouse
Paul and Mabel Thorne

Paul G. Tomlinson
Paul Severing
Percy Brebner
Percy Keese Fitzhugh
Peter B. Kyne
Plato
Quincy Allen
R. Derby Holmes
R. L. Stevenson
R. S. Ball
Rabindranath Tagore
Rahul Alvares
Ralph Bonehill
Ralph Henry Barbour
Ralph Victor
Ralph Waldo Emmerson
Rene Descartes
Ray Cummings
Rex Beach
Rex E. Beach
Richard Harding Davis
Richard Jefferies
Richard Le Gallienne
Robert Barr
Robert Frost
Robert Gordon Anderson
Robert L. Drake
Robert Lansing
Robert Lynd
Robert Michael Ballantyne
Robert W. Chambers
Rosa Nouchette Carey
Rudyard Kipling
Saint Augustine
Samuel B. Allison
Samuel Hopkins Adams
Sarah Bernhardt
Sarah C. Hallowell
Selma Lagerlof
Sherwood Anderson
Sigmund Freud
Standish O'Grady
Stanley Weyman
Stella Benson
Stella M. Francis
Stephen Crane
Stewart Edward White
Stijn Streuvels
Swami Abhedananda
Swami Parmananda
T. S. Ackland

T. S. Arthur
The Princess Der Ling
Thomas A. Janvier
Thomas A Kempis
Thomas Anderton
Thomas Bailey Aldrich
Thomas Bulfinch
Thomas De Quincey
Thomas Dixon
Thomas H. Huxley
Thomas Hardy
Thomas More
Thornton W. Burgess
U. S. Grant
Upton Sinclair
Valentine Williams
Various Authors
Vaughan Kester
Victor Appleton
Victor G. Durham
Victoria Cross
Virginia Woolf
Wadsworth Camp
Walter Camp
Walter Scott
Washington Irving
Wilbur Lawton
Wilkie Collins
Willa Cather
Willard F. Baker
William Dean Howells
William le Queux
W. Makepeace Thackeray
William W. Walter
William Shakespeare
Winston Churchill
Yei Theodora Ozaki
Yogi Ramacharaka
Young E. Allison
Zane Grey

www.ingramcontent.com/pod-product-compliance
Lightning Source LLC
Chambersburg PA
CBHW030323180626
46810CB00003B/1211